The Open
University

A205

Arts: A Second Level Course

Culture and Belief in Europe

1450 – 1600

Block II

Venice and Antwerp

Prepared for the Course Team by
Tim Benton, Stuart Brown,
Noel Coley, David Englander,
David Goodman, Lucille Kekewich,
Catherine King, Diana Norman,
Rosemary O'Day

The Open University

The Open University
Walton Hall,
Milton Keynes
MK7 6AA

First published 1989. Reprinted 1993, 1994. Second edition 1996. Reprinted 1997

Edited, designed and typeset by The Open University

Printed in the United Kingdom by Bell & Bain Ltd., Glasgow

ISBN 0 7492 1167 9

This text is a component of the Open University course A205 *Culture and Belief in Europe 1450–1600*. Details of this and other Open University courses are available from the Central Enquiry Service, The Open University, PO Box 200, Walton Hall, Milton Keynes MK7 6YZ. Tel.: 01908 653078.

2.2

CONTENTS

1 INTRODUCTION

TIM BENTON

Except where stated otherwise, all plate references in this block are to Illustration Book 1.

Having introduced you to the period in Block I, we hope to help you get a feel for it in greater detail by focusing on two cities, their culture, economies, politics, religion and processes of survival and growth. In the first part we begin with general comparisons, first historical and then architectural. By the end of Section 3, you should have a firm grip on the two cities' topography and their most obvious differences. An exercise on the Visual Texts Cassette will prompt you to study the two maps (Maps 1 and 2), and another will guide you through the jungle of architectural styles to establish some basic distinctions and give you a grip on the main style labels (e.g. Gothic, Renaissance, mannerism). TV 5, 'Venice and Antwerp I', contributes to this general introduction by comparing the political and economic centres of both cities. In Section 4 the comparison becomes more analytical in order to answer the question, 'Why was it that Venice survived the many possible causes for disaster, while Antwerp suffered a dramatic collapse?' TV 6, 'Venice and Antwerp II', continues the visual comparison of the two cities, but from the point of view of religion. Radio 4, 'Jews and Christians in Renaissance Venice', investigates the place of Jewry within Venetian society. Both programmes reinforce the arguments of Section 4.

In Part Two the focus changes again. The guilds and confraternities were important sources of stability in both communities, and their patronage of art and architecture affords an insight into their values and priorities. In Sections 6 and 7 we assess the evidence for how ordinary people lived and what they were able to own.

In Part Three the attention turns principally to Venice, although the significance of the case studies is more general. For example, the collection of Greek and Latin manuscripts amassed by Cardinal Bessarion before the Ottoman conquest of Constantinople constitutes an important chapter in the history of the extension of European humanist knowledge. Section 9 takes further the account of the development of printing in Block I and TV 4, 'Plantin', comparing Venice and Antwerp as centres of printing. Section 11 focuses on the intriguing intellectual debts of Friar Francesco Giorgi to the Jewish tradition

of the Cabbala, and Section 10 contextualizes this by outlining the situation of the Jews in Venice. Radio 5, 'Giorgi', looks at another aspect of Giorgi's thought: his exploration of Platonic and Pythagorean proportional theory as applied to an actual building project.

1.1 BLOCK II AND THE THEMES OF THE COURSE

As you make notes on this block, keep the course themes in mind. How does this material relate to the themes? Religion dominated both societies and this is reflected in the block, especially in Sections 4, 5 and 10. You will find plenty of evidence of apparently non-religious activity, but you may want to ask whether this should be used as evidence of increasing secularization during the period. Similarly, the processes by which political authority is established and maintained are pursued throughout the block, and particularly in Sections 2, 4, 5 and 10. In both cities, the looming presence of the superpowers (Spain, France and the Holy Roman Empire) dominated events. And Section 7 provides clear evidence about the limitations of women's situation in the household. Questions about the potential for intellectual innovation and the importance of classical texts underlie all the sections in Part Three. But 'innovation' in this period was just as likely to be restrictive as liberating, whether in politics or in the arts.

1.2 AIMS AND OBJECTIVES

The aims of this block are:

1 To provide you with materials to compare Venice and Antwerp across a range of historical and cultural criteria.

2 To use these materials to test your comprehension of the course themes and ideas and methods introduced in Block I.

After completing this block you should be able to:

1 Make relevant comparisons of the political, economic, social and cultural development of Venice and Antwerp using appropriate evidence.

2 Discuss the course themes and related topics using material supplied in the block.

3 Make judgements about the available evidence, about when and how it is legitimate to use it, either for comparison or in arguments deployed around the course themes.

4   Give an account of the physical shape and characteristic forms of both cities using the maps, illustrations and television programmes.

5   Understand the aspirations and processes of patronage of the guilds and confraternities in both cities.

6   Make observations about the intellectual landscape at the time through the study of Bessarion's collection and the thought of Friar Francesco Giorgi.

7   Cite some specific instances of the interrelationships between minority and dominant communities, and between the ability of men and women to control their immediate surroundings.

PART ONE
COMPARING VENICE AND ANTWERP

2 THE BASIS FOR COMPARISON

TIM BENTON AND DAVID ENGLANDER

2.1 WHY VENICE AND ANTWERP?

Venice and Antwerp were to their age what London and New York are to ours. Each in its heyday occupied the dominant position within the European world economy; each was a cultural and artistic centre of interest and importance. A study of their varying fortunes should therefore be enjoyable and worthwhile.

Both cities were linked by the great European trade routes. Read *KMB*, pp.50–61 and 91–9, and look at Fig. 1.

Figure 1 Map of trade routes in Europe.

EXERCISE

How can Venice's and Antwerp's geographical and economic positions be characterized and differentiated?

DISCUSSION

They occupy strategic positions in the same trading system. Venice, with her naval supremacy in the Adriatic and eastern Mediterranean, had controlled access to the overland spice routes to the East. The rise of the Ottoman Empire in the fifteenth century threatened this ascendency. Antwerp lay on the trade routes linking the Baltic North Sea and Atlantic to the main economic highway of Europe, the Rhine. One effect of the discoveries in the New World, and the sea route to India, was to offer an alternative access to the European markets. Antwerp, with her trade fairs and credit exchanges, was well placed to handle this new trade.

Venice, which reached its apogee in the fifteenth century, was the linchpin in a chain that connected the Levant with northern Europe; Antwerp, its successor, developed during the first half of the sixteenth century into an extraordinary entrepôt, commodity and money market (Fig. 2). At its zenith Antwerp transacted more trade in a fortnight than Venice did in a year. 'I was astonished and wondered much when I beheld Antwerp,' said a rueful Venetian envoy, 'for I saw Venice outdone.'

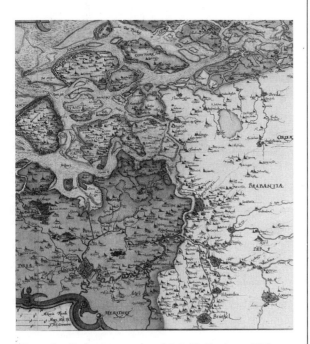

Figure 2   C. Sgrooten, map of Scheldt Estuary, 1573. Section des Manuscrits Ms21596, fol. 18 recto. Copyright Bibliothèque Royale Albert 1er, Brussels.

In social structure, Venice and Antwerp had much in common. Venice, with its 190,000 inhabitants, was the larger of the two; Antwerp's population, though just over half the size of its rival, was nevertheless sufficient to place it among the top half-dozen of European cities. Both were socially diverse. Both possessed a proletariat, a bourgeoisie and a ruling patriciate.

2.2   VENICE IN THE SIXTEENTH CENTURY

Venice in the sixteenth century was at the centre of a land empire which stretched from Bergamo near Milan to the eastern Mediterranean. Read *KMB,* pp.103–6.

Traditionally, the Venetian Empire had been controlled by merchant families who shared in government but were not too proud to engage in trade. The 'republican' virtues embodying this spirit were constantly referred to by Venetian orators, ever ready to detect an enfeeblement of the people's resolve.

Venice proved remarkably resourceful in responding to the expansion of the Ottoman Empire and the new Atlantic trade routes. When the Venetian ports along the southern Dalmatian coast and in the eastern Mediterranean fell, one by one, to the Turks, the Venetians simply switched to trading with the new rulers. Similarly, the new Portuguese trade routes to India and the Spice Islands did nothing to stem the flow of pepper to Venice. If anything, this trade increased as Indian merchants switched to overland routes to escape harassment by the Portuguese ships. Venice developed new trade routes through Alexandria. And the acute dependence of the Venetians on imported food was relieved by the rapid build-up of mainland possessions in northern Italy. Soon the Venetian families administered some of the most advanced and productive farms in Italy, and by 1600 Venice was virtually self-sufficient in foodstuffs.

2.3   ANTWERP IN THE SIXTEENTH CENTURY

Antwerp's rapid growth was dependent on two inescapable factors: the support of the Spanish king and the open access of the river Scheldt to the sea. In the end, these two factors came into conflict during the uprising of the Protestant Dutch. Read *KMB,* pp.311–18.

The impact of these events on Antwerp must be followed more closely. From the late 1550s, more and more **Anabaptists** and **Calvinists** were executed. By 1566 thousands of poor and artisan Calvinists regularly collected in the fields outside the walls to hear the 'hedge preachers' (Fig. 3). In 1566 William of Orange began to offer a measure of religious toleration. A spate of image-breaking was inaugurated in August by the smashing of stained glass windows and destruction of 'idols' in the churches and monasteries. William made 'Accords' with the different religious groups, allowing them to worship in their own churches or meeting-houses.

In 1567 Orange left, and an imperial garrison was installed. A massive citadel was built outside the walls (Fig. 4), and from 1567 to 1573 Alva clamped down on heresy with fearful efficiency, but he could not stamp it out. Nor could trade be kept open against the depradations of the Sea Beggars.

The events of the Spanish Fury in 1576 followed inevitably from the juxtaposition of the unpaid Catholic **tercios** bottled up in the citadel and a city which was looking increasingly to the Protestant Dutch for salvation, without whose help all sea-borne trade was blocked.

When a small group of Protestant troops from the States General entered Antwerp, the Spanish troops burst out of the citadel and ran amok for three days and nights. Six or seven thousand soldiers died along with an uncertain number of civilians (Fig. 6). The new town hall and many of the guild houses were set alight (Fig. 7).

Figure 4 Frans Hogenberg, The citadel, c.1567, *engraving, 19 × 27.5 cm. Copyright Museum Plantin-Moretus/Print Room, Antwerp III/H.138.*

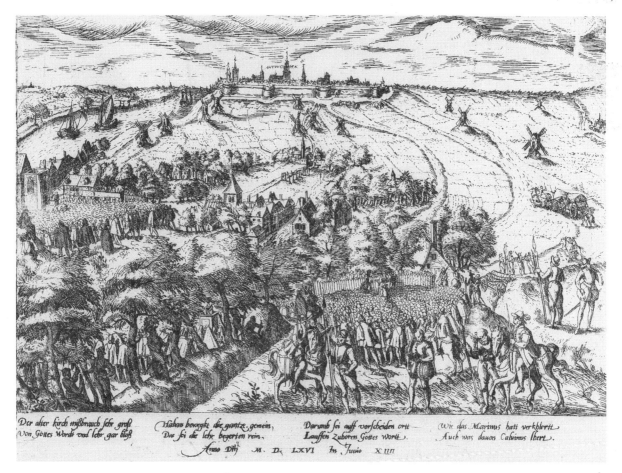

Figure 3 Frans Hogenberg, Hedge preachers at Antwerp, 1566, *engraving, 21 × 28 cm. On the left Lutherans, in the middle Walloon Calvinists, and on the right Dutch-speaking Calvinists. Copyright Museum Plantin-Moretus/Print Room, Antwerp III/H.70/3.*

Figure 5   Frans Hogenberg, German mercenaries driven out of the New Town, *2 August 1577, engraving, 21 × 28 cm. Note the house of the Eesterlings. Copyright Museum Plantin-Moretus/Print Room, Antwerp III/H.101/4.*

Don John of Austria, the new Governor of the Netherlands, was sent to make peace. In 1577 the States General agreed the 'Perpetual Accord' with Don John, by which he agreed to withdraw his troops (Fig. 5) and accept the privileges of the states in exchange for allegiance. The citadel was demolished and trade along the Scheldt reopened. An uneasy period followed, with Orange, now a Calvinist, sharing power with the Catholic Archduke Mathias, the new Governor General. The **Jesuits** and Grey Friars (Franciscans) were expelled from Antwerp and a 'Religious Peace' signed in 1578 allowing Catholics, Lutherans and Calvinists to worship freely, the available churches and monasteries being divided amongst them. In 1581 Catholics were forbidden to worship openly in any of the churches in Antwerp.

An attempt was made to seek the protection of the Duke of Anjou, son of Catherine de' Medici. In February 1582 he arrived, bringing with him the futile expectation of marriage to Queen Elizabeth of England and a guarantee to protect the Religious Peace. The trappings of this particularly empty 'joyous entry' have been recorded in an engraving by Hogenberg

(see *Illustration Book 2*, TBC 2A, **Pl.2**, p.36). His engravings of this event are discussed in TBC 2A.

Twenty years of precarious survival on this tightrope (1566–85) ended definitively when Alessandro Farnese, the Duke of Parma, recaptured Antwerp for the Spanish and Catholicism. Nearly half of Antwerp's population left for the Protestant North.

Figure 6   Frans Hogenberg, Episode from the Spanish Fury, *1576, engraving, 21 × 28 cm. Copyright Museum Plantin-Moretus/Print Room, Antwerp III/H.99/6.*

Figure 7   Frans Hogenberg, Spanish Fury and town hall, 4 November 1576, *engraving, 21 × 28 cm. Members of the military guilds engage the Spanish troups in a last ditch struggle. The Stadhuis and many of the guild houses were set on fire. Copyright Museum Plantin-Moretus/Print Room, Antwerp III/H.99/5.*

2.4   GOVERNMENT (VENICE AND ANTWERP COMPARED)

The Venetians were particularly proud of the mixed form of government that obtained within the republic which, it was asserted, was the perfect embodiment of Platonic theory. Contemporaries were convinced that in the perfection of the constitution lay the secret of Venetian liberty and stability. It was, however, an open secret. Gasparo Contarini's *The Commonwealth and Government of Venice* (1534) was a treatise on republican freedom which presented the Venetian Republic as the state of liberty, superior even to ancient Athens and Rome.

EXERCISE

Read his account (*Anthology* II.1) and then, in a couple of paragraphs, explain how the author tries to relate the structure of government to the alleged absence of internal social conflict.

DISCUSSION

Contarini's account presents Venetian government as a pyramidal structure with the Great Council at the base and the doge at the

apex. The Great Council, the sovereign body of all adult male patricians, elected the office-holders who filled the numerous magistracies and administrative boards that were responsible for the day-to-day management of public affairs. The Great Council, with its 2,000-odd members, was, however, too large and too unwieldy to initiate policy or act with speed and secrecy in international affairs. Real power was located elsewhere – in the Senate, an altogether smaller and more select body; in the 'colledge' or Collegio, which set its agenda; and above all in the Council of Ten, a standing committee of public safety which was responsible for all matters affecting state security, including issues of war and peace. The duty of the doge, who held office for life, was to supply the co-ordination necessary to ensure the smooth functioning of a diffuse system of government which, in order to check the growth of personal power, relied upon rapid rotation of office within a complex of countervailing committees and councils of state.

The strength of the Venetian constitution, according to Contarini, lay in the division of power between its constituent parts. In his account the doge represents the monarchical element, the Senate the aristocratic element, and the Great Council the democratic element. Democracy, however, did not entail mass representation in the governmental process. The exclusion of the common people was, in fact, taken as axiomatic. Political participation was confined to a legally defined nobility who comprised less than 2 per cent of the population of Venice. Membership of the Great Council – the necessary qualification for entry into the city magistracies, naval commands, embassies and governorships of subject dominions – was in practice the prerogative of a hereditary caste. Similarly, Venetian liberty, as Contarini conceived it, referred to freedom from foreign domination rather than freedom from want. The celebrated mixed constitution was, in any case, a myth. Jean Bodin, whom we shall encounter in Block VII, subsequently argued that Venetian government was aristocratic in composition and oligarchic in form. Contarini's eulogizing account of the skill and insight displayed by the Venetian patriciate in the management of affairs was not, however, questioned. To its restraint and prudence, its commitment to the rule of law, its well-stocked granaries, and its statecraft in supporting institutions that satisfied popular ambitions within an approved framework – for example, the permanent civil service (staffed exclusively by middle-class citizens) or the trades guilds and charitable and religious fraternities – can be traced the means by which the Venetian aristocracy sustained its power.

EXERCISE

How does the government of Venice compare with that of Antwerp? Read now the extract from Guicciardini's *Description of the Low Countries* (*Anthology* II.2), and summarize such similarities and differences as you observe.

DISCUSSION

Guicciardini's account suggests a number of contrasts in the status of the two communities, in the structure of government, in the range of functions performed by the ruling élites, and in the material base of patrician power.

One obvious difference concerns size. Antwerp was administered by an eighteen-strong aldermanic college assisted by a handful of permanent officials. Dissimilarities in size and scale of government operations in this case reflected the different status of the two communes. In spite of the senatorial structure of government, the Antwerpers had no imperial pretensions. Although public

buildings often bore the insignia **SPQA** (*Senatus Populusque Antwerpiensis*), office-holding was of a civic rather than an imperial character. In the course of the fifteenth century the city fathers of Antwerp had extended representation to the *pooterij*, the wealthy burgesses, to secure patrician interests against guild encroachments. These concessions, which were not revoked once the crisis had passed, ensured that property was well protected in the town hall. Power nevertheless remained firmly in the grip of the patriciates. Representatives of the rich burgesses were appointed to the Broad Council – two from each of the twelve wards into which the city was divided – to serve for a two-year term under four headmen, who were also recruited from local notables and appointed by the magistrates.

On the face of it the dissimilarities seem to be so great as to render comparison invidious. Venice, after all, was an independent city-state, a maritime republic exercising dominion over much of the mainland, with substantial colonial possessions and a formidable navy to protect them. Antwerp, by contrast, was merely a ducal dependency, a fragment within the far-flung Spanish Empire whose supreme ruler also held the duchy of Brabant. Ducal rights, institutionalized within Antwerp's administration, were, however, more apparent than real. The duke was represented by the *burgrave*, but by the mid-sixteenth century this, as Guicciardini notes, was largely an honorific post. The two chief legal officers – the *margrave* or *schout*, who was in charge of criminal justice, and the *amptmann* or *amman*, who was responsible for civil disputes – were also ducal appointees. But once again, as Guicciardini tells us, their authority was limited by the privileges of the city since the power of arrest required the approval of one of Antwerp's two burgomasters. The aldermanic college, though it required external approval, had, by our period, also become largely self-selecting. 'In contrast to the many other towns where the magistrature was the arbitrary creation of the sovereign prince,' writes Leon Voet (1973), 'the duke's right of appointment became no more than a fiction in Antwerp.'

2.5 MYTHS AND TRADITIONS

From the medieval period onwards, Venetian historians and rulers consciously evoked traditions of Venetian 'freedoms' and of its inalienable rights to international power.

Among the themes treated were legends attributing divine approval of the city through the mediation of the relics of St Mark and pseudo-historical myths attributing semi-imperial status to the Venetian doge, on a par with the pope and the Holy Roman Emperor.

In 828/9, so legend relates, two Venetian merchants stole the remains of St Mark from Alexandria and brought them back to Venice. This episode, known as the *translatio*, was of great importance in Venetian history because it incorporated a myth which linked the republic directly to the sources of Christianity, just as the martyrdom of St Peter was linked to the founding of the Roman Church. A prominent set of thirteenth-century mosaics in the lunettes of the portals of the façade of St Mark's represented these events. One remains on the left-most portal of the façade (see **Pl. 1**, p.26). A procession carries the body of St Mark in front of an already recognizable depiction of the basilica of St Mark's. Every year, on the feast of St Mark, a similar procession would wind its way around the Piazza San Marco, re-enacting this scene. We can see the full set in Gentile Bellini's *Procession in Piazza San Marco* (1496) (**Pl. 2**, p.26).

Central to Venetian imperial mythology was the story of Pope Alexander III and Emperor Frederick Barbarossa. Pope Alexander III had taken refuge in Venice in the convent of Santa Maria della Carità in 1177 to escape the military invasion of the German emperor. In gratitude to the doge, who protected him and waged war successfully on the emperor, the pope granted a number of symbolic marks of authority: a white candle denoting love and faith, a sword commemorating the defence of the papacy and, most evocatively of all, a golden ring with which the doge was to marry the sea each year as a sign of Venetian naval supremacy.

After the Venetian naval victory over the emperor, Frederick Barbarossa travelled to Venice and prostrated himself at the feet of the pope in front of St Mark's. The pope then granted a perpetual indulgence at St Mark's during the feast of the Ascension. On the subsequent trip to Rome, the doge was also granted the right to be shaded by a ceremonial umbrella, like the pope and emperor.

The events of 1177 provided the raw material for the deliberate exploitation of a myth of Venetian authority. Every year on the feast of the Ascension (the *Sensa*), the doge would perform the *Desponsatio*, the ceremony of the marriage with the sea. After a religious service and an elaborate procession, the doge was rowed out into the lagoon on a fabulously decorated barge – known as the *Bucintoro* – and there cast a gold ring into the sea, fulfilling Pope Alexander's wish that 'you should marry the sea, just as a man marries his wife in sign of perpetual domination'. A ceremony which had begun as a traditional benediction of the sea at the opening of the trading season had become transformed into a potent assertion of naval power backed by papal authority.

But the status of these symbols and ceremonies could not suffice alone. The populace and visiting dignitaries had to have the historical justifications asserted and demonstrated in cycles of painting in all the public buildings. The stories which composed the 'history' of Pope Alexander III and the Emperor Barbarossa were depicted in three successive cycles in the Great Council Hall of the ducal palace (*c*.1365–1419, 1475–1564 and 1577–1600). The surviving set, painted after the great fire of 1577, includes the episode where the pope and doge receive the emperor's son Otto, who has offered to negotiate the truce (**Pl. 3**, p.27).

By contrast, the myths growing up around the origins of Antwerp were characteristic of the misty legends of survival in Dark Age Europe. A giant named Druon Antigonus was supposed to have ruled here, exacting tolls from the passing river trade. Salvius Brabo, Lord of Tongres (supposedly related to Julius Caesar by marriage), slew Antigonus and came to Antwerp to fling the giant's hand into the Scheldt.

Whatever the truth behind this story, it symbolically brings together external power (the link with the Roman Empire) and the river, just as the legend of the ring of St Mark associates the lagoon (and Venetian maritime power) with the authority of St Mark and the validation of the pope.

In Antwerp the tradition of the 'Joyous Entry' of each new ruler, when the new *margrave* or regent was supposed to perform the ceremony of recognizing the charters and freedoms of the city, was celebrated in frequent woodcuts, engravings and written accounts.

2.6 ALLEGORY OF COMMERCE

For a vivid insight into the commercial world of the merchants who united Venice and Antwerp by their trade, look at **Pl. 4a** (p.28). This woodcut was conceived as an allegory of commerce for commercial reproduction, presumably aimed at a prestigious clientele of international merchants who would fill in the various empty spaces on the woodcut with their own mottoes and devices. Johann Neudörfer, who died in 1563, is credited with the composition, but the plate was first published in Augsburg in 1585. Neudörfer was a mathematician and accountant who is credited with having introduced the **Fugger** family to double-entry book-keeping.

The image is based on an elaborate humanist structure combining allegories of virtues and vices with a realistic background showing Antwerp and a composition which contrasts debt (on the left) with credit (on the right). Along the top are shown the arms of all the European cities with international fairs. In the middle is a great fountain bearing the names of the main trading commodities. Above this is a column bearing a 'Zornal' or Journal of Accounts, which in turn supports the figure of Chance. Above is Mercury, the god of commerce, with scales weighing debt against credit. All around, at this upper level, are the hazards of international trade. Sea and land battles, highwaymen, dishonest middlemen, fire and death are portrayed on the debtor side.

Down below, two commercial enterprises are contrasted, presided over by Fortune and witnessed by Good Faith, Liberty, Integrity, Knowledge of languages and Discretion. The two clerks on the left are keeping the treasury ledger (see **Pl. 4b**, p.29, for detail). In the middle, two men on the right show their ability to keep their secrets and remain silent ('Taciturnitas'); one of them is biting his thumb (see **Pl. 4c**, p.29, for detail). On the other side are two agents, dressed as Turks, labelled 'Knowledge of languages' (see **Pl. 4b** for detail). On the right-hand side, we see goods being packed and labelled, while a clerk keeps a ledger in double-entry book-keeping. Note the large quantity of coins on the counting table. In two inner rooms, agents and clerks count coins and record details of transactions, while, on the far right, an old man surrounded by signs of great wealth gives instructions to a young man (perhaps his son or a factor). On the left, the signs are less good. There is no cash in sight, and the merchants in the inner rooms seem to be arguing over a debt or gesticulating over the weight of a barrel of goods.

This print represents a view of the most up-to-date commercial practice. The period of its conception and printing spans the period of Antwerp's agony and decline. How far we should read religious meanings into the scholarly and moralizing imagery is an open question. But it does bring home very strongly the sense of danger and imminent disaster which haunted trade and commerce in the sixteenth century.

3 URBAN CHANGE AND BUILDING TYPES

TIM BENTON

3.1 TWO BIRD'S EYE VIEWS

Look at Fig. 8 and Maps 1 and 2. The Barbari map of Venice is dated 1500, and consists of six large woodcuts making an image measuring 134.5 × 281.8 cm. The original request to make the map was made by a German merchant, Antonio Kolb. The view is from the south with the sea behind us and the mainland ahead. We have reproduced only the central section in Map 1.

The Boloniensis map of Antwerp (Map 2) is one of several based on the copper engraving by Hieronymous Cock of 1557. The view is from the east towards the Scheldt. The Boloniensis woodcut was published in 1565 and measures 120 × 265 cm. There were twenty blocks instead of the six that Barbari used.

Please spend half an hour now on the maps exercise on Side B, band 3 of the Visual Texts Cassette, identifying the various key places on each map. First read the accompanying notes in the *Cassette Handbook*. You will also find TV 5 of help to you at this stage, since it provides a comparative guide to the two cities.

It should be clear from this exercise that both cities shared certain key features (ceremonial and commercial centres, ports, ship building and other industrial areas, storage facilities and so on). Furthermore, both cities relied on canals for much of their internal distribution. But the most obvious features of comparison are the differences between the cities. Venice's situation is unique for a city of this size, while Antwerp is organized like many other European trading cities.

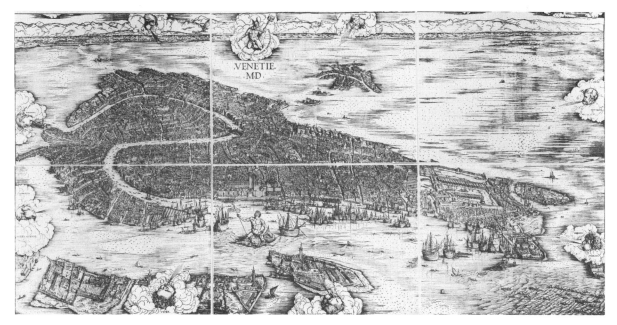

Figure 8   Jacopo de' Barbari, map of Venice, 1500, wood engraving, 134.5 × 281.8 cm. British Museum Department of Prints and Drawings.

3.2 ANTWERP (URBAN DEVELOPMENT)

Look at Figs 9–11.

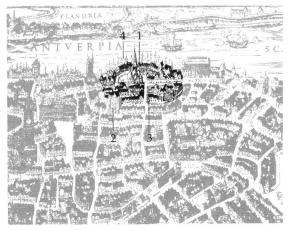

1	St Walburgiskerk	3	Vierschaar
2	Vleeshuis	4	Old Wharf

Figure 9   Plan of the Burcht, Antwerp, c.1000.

Look at Fig. 9 and Map 2. This was a typical form for a medieval fortified town, clustered around the Burcht (or castle enclosure). The line of the walls and moat can clearly be seen running from the fish market (I1 bottom right) past the Vleeshuis (J2 top left) to the large gun emplacement in K1. You can even see a section of the eleventh-century walls (K2 top left corner).

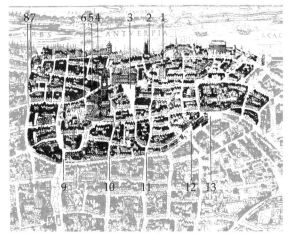

1	Vleeshuis	8	Kammerpoort
2	Steen castle	9	Meirpoort
3	Grote Markt	10	Sint-Katelijnepoort
4	Onze Lieve Vrouw	11	Wijngaardpoort
5	Hoogstraat	12	Minnenbrug
6	Oude Kornmarkt	13	Koepoort
7	Sint-Jorispoort		

Figure 10   Antwerp, showing the first to third extensions of the city.

Over the next four centuries the city expanded in four main phases, each one contained within a new circle of walls. The eleventh-century extension was motivated by the need to include the large swathe of suburbs which had grown up around the church of Our Lady

1	Kronenburgpoort	7	Kipdorp
2	Begijnhof	8	Kipdorppoort
3	Sint-Jorispoort	9	Sint-Jacobskerk
4	New Exchange	10	Rode Poort
5	Meir	11	Slijkpoort
6	lange Nieuwstraat	12	Posterneppoort

Figure 11   Antwerp, fourth extension 1314–1400.

(H2–H3 Onze Lieve Vrouw) and the monastery to the north (K2 'Monasterium predicatorum'). Try to trace the line of these walls and moat on the Boloniensis (Map 2). Many of the old gates and bridges across the moat are preserved in the names of squares (e.g. K3 'Pons Vaccaius', also known as the Koepoortbrug, i.e. Cow Gate Bridge). The bulge around I3–J3 incorporated the important Engelse Beurs or English Exchange (J3) and the Old Weigh House (J3).

The second extension, around 1250, reflected the economic development of the city and its growing independence from external control, although the Burcht remained as a completely fortified and separate stronghold for the *burgrave*. The main emphasis of the city was shifting southwards (with the main gates of the city, at this stage, being the Kammerpoort to the south corner of F2–3 and G2–3 and the three main eastern gates: the Meirpoort or Meirbrug (G4), the Sint Katelijnepoort (H4) and the Wijngaardpoort). In the later extensions to the east, these gates provided the line for the main streets of the city: respectively, the Kammerstraat, the Meir (where the fairs were held), the lange

Nieuwstraat and the Kipdorp.

In 1314 a new line of walls was begun, and following an enlargement to the north in 1374, these now followed more or less the line occupied by the sixteenth-century fortifications shown on the Boloniensis plan. From this point onwards, the basic area of the city did not vary much, although the population continued to expand from c.10,000 in 1358 to 18,000 in 1374 and 20,000 in 1394. From 1496 to 1568 the population grew from c.47,000 to 100,259. In consequence, land prices were forced up and housing became increasingly densely packed.

In 1520 a plan for the improvement of the fortifications was drawn up. On 10 May 1540 the designs of Donato Buoni de Pellezuoli were approved and work began, to be completed in 1555. In Fig. 12 you can see the first and largest of the five new gates being built, the Sint-Jorispoort, which was sometimes called the Keizerpoort in honour of Emperor Charles V (C5 'Porta Caesarea'). The style is that of the Venetian architect and fortifications engineer Michele Sanmichele (**Pl. 5**, p.30). The old fourteenth-century walls with their high towers (vulnerable to cannon fire) can be seen encircling the rest of the city. The new walls were built on modern principles, incorporating low projecting bastions from which cannon fire could be used to cover the straight stretches of curtain walls in between. If any of the bastions were to fall, they were in turn covered by raised gun platforms (cavaliers) on top of the gates and in towers in the middle of the curtain walls. If you look at how the cannon are disposed in the Boloniensis, the system is self-evident.

An investment of this kind entailed the risk of limiting the further growth of the city within the ring of walls. As it is, access was severely limited by the restriction in the number of gates. To allow for expansion, a 'new town' (Nieuwstad) was provided to the north, consisting of an empty swampy area enclosed by walls (Map 2). The role of a young politician and brewer Gilbert Van Schoonbeke in trying to develop this area is discussed in TV 5. The vacant plots in the new town had barely begun to fill up when the city entered its long period of stagnation after the 1580s.

The citadel which Alva built to the south of the city led to the demolition of the walls on this side. Although the citadel was partly demolished after the Spanish Fury (see Fig. 13), it was rebuilt after the fall of Antwerp to Farnese. The function of the citadel was to keep its citizens in order and the city loyal. Albert and Isabella were received first in the citadel (Fig. 14); if you look at the guns of the citadel, they're trained on the city rather than away to the south.

Figure 13 H. Wierix, engraving of demolition of the northern walls of the citadel in August 1577, from Recueil de 112 gravures réprésentant … du Duc d'Albe. Copyright Museum Plantin-Moretus/Print Room, Antwerp R.194.

We can summarize the growth of Antwerp as a series of interactions between commercially driven growth within the constraints imposed by the need for defensive walls and an externally imposed garrison. The functions which, in the origins of the city, had been

Figure 12 Bird's eye view of Antwerp from the south, c.1545, from the Chronicle of Lodewijk van Cauckerken (1629–1704). Copyright Bibliothèque Royale Albert 1er, Brussels.

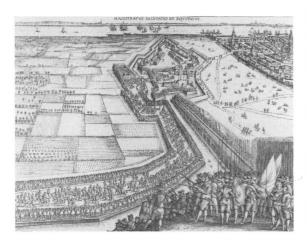

Figure 14 Pieter van der Borcht, The magistrates of Antwerp come out to greet Albert and Isabella, *from J. Bochius,* Historica narratio profectionis et inaugurationis … Antwerpen, *1602 Inv. 17.932– 17.931. Copyright Museum Plantin-Moretus/Print Room, Antwerp R.45.1.*

exercised by the Steen and the fortified Burcht were replaced by the citadel.

3.3 VENICE (URBAN DEVELOPMENT)

The development of Venice was controlled by the hydrographic laws of the Venetian lagoon (see Fig. 15). The screen of sandbanks running roughly north from Chioggia to the Lido di

Jesolo partly protected a large area of shallow water fed by several rivers. These rivers carved grooves in the mud which channelled their paths invisibly through the lagoon just as if they were still on the mainland. Three gaps in the sandbank (Chioggia, Malamocco and Lido) allowed access to the lagoon from the sea. Where the sea tides met the flow from the rivers, banks of mud were formed and one of these interchanges is the site of Venice.

The first settlements on the mud banks around the estuary of the Marzenego river (which becomes the Grand Canal) date from the seventh century. Unlike Antwerp, which began as a fortified nucleus and expanded outwards, the full area of Venice was spanned by the first islands, although considerable infilling was later carried out. (Look at Figs 17 and 18.) San Pietro in Castello to the east and S. Nicolo dei Mendicoli to the west were among the first churches to be founded. Notice how the scattering of islands, each with its parish church, slowly clumps together to form modern Venice. As the city filled in the stretches of water dividing the islands, a network of canals was formed.

The parishes, divided by canals, retained much of the independence of their original island form; most were linked to their neighbours by only one bridge in each direction and these bridges more usually lie along the axis of an open space, or campo, or in the middle of an 'island'.

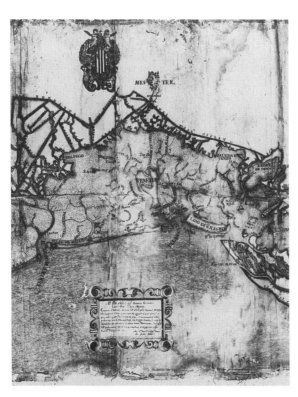

Figure 15 Sebastiano Alberti, Laguna de Venezia. *Biblioteca Museo Correr MS P.D. c.856. Photo: Giacomelli.*

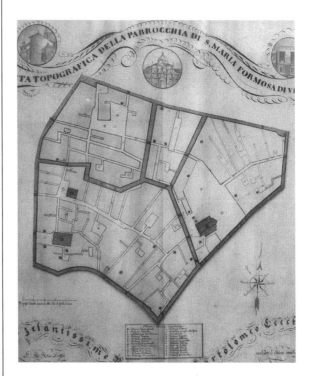

Figure 16 Nineteenth-century plan of parish of Santa Maria Formosa. Photo: Tim Benton.

Figure 17   Map of Venice in the twelfth century.

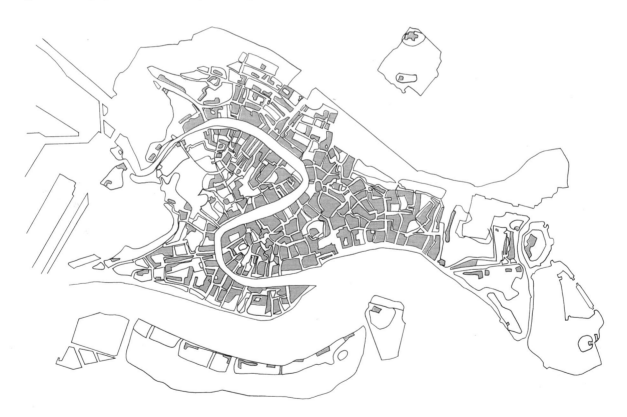

Figure 18   Map of Venice early fourteenth century.

———— EXERCISE ————

Look at the Barbari map (Map 1) and, with the aid of Fig. 16, see if you can trace the survival of some of the original 'islands' in the network of canals. Remember each island had its own parish church.

———— DISCUSSION ————

The easiest examples to spot on the Barbari map are Santa Maria Formosa (I4–J4), SS Apostoli (G2), San Giacomo del Orio (D2), San Toma (D3), Sant'Aponal (E3), Sant'Angelo (C4). In many cases today the original churches have either been destroyed (as in the case of Sant'Angelo) or moved, but the Barbari map shows the arrangement well. In each campo you can see one or two wells, each with the distinctive pattern of a central marble well-head flanked by four stone drains linked to the well-head by diagonal lines.

3.4 URBAN TYPES IN VENICE

Take the Campo Santa Maria Formosa. Look at Fig. 16 and **Pl. 6** (p.30). The existing parish can be thought of as one large island subdivided into four by canals. Originally, however, there were three parish churches, each with its own 'island'.

Each of the 'islands' has one or more pedestrian routes running through the middle, with houses, narrow lanes and yards running back to the canals. A clear example is the *calle lunga* (long street) which runs into the Campo Santa Maria Formosa from the north.

Another example of a very early pedestrian thoroughfare is the Salizzada San Lio (**Pl. 10**, p.32). The importance of the Salizzada San Lio derives from the proximity to the Rialto Bridge. One of the streets leading off the Salizzada San Lio is the Calle del Paradiso, which, with its timber jettied shops, represents a very old type of Venetian street (**Pl. 8**, p.31). This one was a speculative development intitiated in 1417 by the abbot of Pomposa and passed on to families of the purest patrician stock. The decorative arch at one end (**Pl. 9**, p.31) records the foundation with the Foscari and Mocenigo arms.

Much of the building development in Venice was the result of wealthy families investing in land which they owned or which they bought for profit either as shops and workshops or simply for housing. A sixteenth-century example of speculative housing and shops can

also be found in this parish in the Campo Santa Marina (**Pl. 11**, p.32). In this case, the two blocks, linked by an arch, were each divided into four apartments. Shops were provided for rent on the ground floor but there is no link to a canal.

Canals in Venice are of three main kinds. Some retain the curving form of the 'natural' rivers and channels progressively encroached on to form the boundaries to the 'islands'. Others follow the pattern of drainage ditches, which was an essential function in the drying out of the swampy patches in between the 'islands'. Others again are laid out geometrically like streets in a city. These are characteristic of the areas laid out on newly colonized mud banks on the northern side of the city. Some of these, like the Fondamenta degli Ormesini, are provided with continuous quays along one or both sides (**Pl. 12**, p.32). In most cases, a campo is served directly by a rio. Follow the line of the rio from San Zan Degola in the north to San Polo in the south (C2–D3). You can clearly see four parish churches, with their campi, deployed along this important axis.

Canal access to the campi was necessary for ceremonial reasons and to give access to the 'island' from outside. Most campi had at least one confraternity building in it and, associated with the confraternity, a flagpole. From here on the appropriate feast days processions would set off along the canals, usually finishing up in the Piazza San Marco. Attached to the church of Santa Maria Formosa were several confraternity meeting houses, of which the most important was the bombardiers (**Pl. 7**, p.31). The link with the Arsenal was reflected in the patronage of the Cappello family, who paid for one of the façades in honour of their relative Admiral Vincenzo Cappello (1542). Two of the other confraternities were the fruiterers and the *casselleri* (makers of bridal chests). The church is shown in TV 6.

Looking again at the Barbari map, can you see where some of the big monastic establishments were? Most monasteries are founded on the outskirts of the built-up area (this holds for Antwerp as much as Venice). Two of the biggest Venetian monasteries were the Franciscan Frari (B3 top) and the Dominican SS Giovanni e Paolo (J3). In both cases, there is a large campo facing onto a rio with plenty of space for embarking processions. There is also, in each case, a *Scuola Grande*, one of the six major confraternity houses (San Rocco in the case of the Frari and San Marco in the case of SS Giovanni e Paolo) (see **Pl. 13**, p.32). The latter church was where most of the doges were buried and where some of the most splendid late **Gothic** and early Renaissance wall tombs are to be found. You can see on the Barbari map how wide steps were provided to give access to the canal. Other monasteries can be found at L4 (San Lorenzo, Benedictine), C6 (Abbey of San Gregorio, Benedictine), and C4 left (Santo Stefano, Eremitani).

The commercial heart of Venice was the Rialto (F3) (**Pl. 14**, p.33). A devastating fire in 1514 led to a rebuilding of the whole area. The buildings which the architects Scarpagnino and, later, Sansovino provided for the market are illustrated in TV 5. In the Barbari map you can see the old wooden Rialto Bridge, which also featured in Carpaccio's painting (see **Col. Pl. 6**, p.119). The decision to build a new stone bridge was only taken in the 1580s; the architect was an engineer, Antonio da Ponte, who managed to cover the full 28 metres span with one arch. The design allowed the great ceremonial vessels like the *Bucintoro* to pass through without the need for a drawbridge.

The ceremonial heart of Venice is the Piazza San Marco. Until the eleventh century the Palazzo Ducale was surrounded on all sides by water. During the twelfth century the Palazzo Ducale was rebuilt on a larger scale, roughly on the present site, and a new and enlarged St Mark's was begun. Along the north side of the piazza were shops and offices which, in 1514, were rebuilt in a similar style (**Pl. 15**, p.33). Despite the scale of these undertakings, the style used was innately conservative. The elevation design of the Palazzo Ducale with its tracery of Gothic arches, which had been begun on the southern side, was continued round the west side facing the piazzetta and only completed in 1424. Most of the additions to the Palazzo Ducale in the fifteenth and sixteenth centuries were designed to blend in as well as possible to the existing building (**Pl. 16**, p.34). Subsequent changes are discussed in TV 5.

Among the essential organs of state were the customs house and salt warehouses (D7–E7) and several state granaries, of which the largest were right next to the Zecca (G6–H6). These granaries were needed not only to store food for times of hunger, but more urgently for the provisioning of the large crews which rowed and sailed across the eastern Mediterranean. The Venetian Republic had rigorous laws imposing quarantine on the whole population whenever contagious diseases were brought into the city. Reserves of food were essential to enforce these laws.

The foreign trading communities such as the Germans, Turks and Greeks were also provided with amenities to encourage them to keep their business in Venice. The Fondaco dei Tedeschi (**Pl. 17**, p.34) was originally decorated with famous frescoes by Giorgione and others. It provided accommodation for storage and people. Inside, it consisted of a huge courtyard lined with several storeys of arcades. The same basic form was used in the Hansa house built for the German merchant community in Antwerp in the 1560s. This form was also used increasingly for Exchanges all over Europe, beginning with the Antwerp Exchange.

The evolution of the Venetian palazzo is a complex one. By the thirteenth century a type had developed known as a fondaco, consisting of a large frontage with living quarters flanking an arcaded central section whose function was primarily for storage and business (**Pl. 19**, p.35). Variations on this theme (**Pl. 20**, p.36) retained the arches giving access to the *androne* or hallway at ground level and the row of colonnaded windows lighting the first floor living area, but they adapted to the site and abandoned symmetry. The Gothic variants of this type provide the majority of examples visible in the Barbari map. Look at **Pl. 18** (p.35). This key site on the bend of the Grand Canal can clearly be seen on the Barbari map (A3–A4). The Foscari palace was built by Doge Francesco Foscari in 1452. The Giustinian palaces were added. These great houses have evolved from the functional commercial centres of the fondaco type into almost purely ceremonial palaces. But they retain the tripartite arrangement with the main living area in the middle and large hallways below, which were still sometimes used for storage. During the second half of the sixteenth century, Renaissance forms and principles began to penetrate Venetian architectural circles without seriously affecting the traditional layout. Sanmichele designed a sumptuous palace for Girolamo Grimani in 1556 (**Pl. 21**, p.36) which took twenty years to complete. Although the façade is treated in classical terms, the tripartite organization is still visible, especially at the lower level, where the *androne* is articulated like a triumphal arch.

To grasp the stylistic implications of these changes, spend half an hour now on the architectural style exercise on Side B, band 4 of the Visual Texts Cassette. First read the accompanying notes in the *Cassette Handbook*.

3.5 URBAN TYPES IN ANTWERP

In the Antwerp of 1540–85 land values and house prices were exceptionally high. The pressure on land within the circle of walls was principally met by subdividing monastic or private properties and building even more houses on the sites. The houses of the wealthy merchants can often be identified on the Boloniensis (Map 2) by their towers, from which a look-out could be kept for the arrival of ships on the Scheldt. One such mansion, the Van Liere house, which was sold to the English nation in 1551–2, can be seen on K5. Another, the residence of the fabulously wealthy Fugger family of German bankers, can be seen on the right of F2, again identified by its tower. The style of most of these houses was conservative, retaining Gothic forms (**Pl. 22**, p.37). Large monasteries like St Michael's Abbey (E1) or the Minderbroeders (K4 marked 'Minorita') which had lain outside the walls were enclosed by the new city. Other patches of open space were provided by the almshouses and hospitals such as the Sint Elisabethgasthuis (D5), which – with the neighbouring girls' orphanage, the Maagdenhuis (E4 bottom) – provided a whole city block devoted to social care (**Pl. 23**, p.37). Another similar area was in the north-east corner of the city near the Rode Poort (M6), where we find both the Begijnhof (K6–K7) and the almshouse and infirmary of the Zeven Bloedstortingen (L6).

In the new quarters of the city, wealthy parishioners contributed to the construction of large parish churches such as Sint Jacobskerk (I5–I6) (**Pls 24, 25**, p.38), Sint Andrieskerk (E2) or Sint Joriskerk (C4). Interspersed between these large organizations were innumerable examples of the Godshuis, typically containing a chapel and charitable housing for a few dozen old people. One such can be seen on the former Falconrei Canal, the Godshuis Jan Van DerBiest (M4, middle), scarcely distinguishable from the houses around it (**Pl. 26**, p.39). Slightly more visible as a church was the Sint Annakapel en Godshuis (J4 bottom, middle) (**Pl. 27**, p.39), which is discussed in TV 6. Most of these were founded by individual men or women.

Legislation passed in 1545 banned the use of timber alone in the building of houses, and the pace of the sixteenth-century building boom is attested to by the fact that no unrestored wooden houses survive in the city centre (Fig. 19 and **Pl. 28**, p.40). Most of the new housing was quickly and cheaply built of brick with limestone lintels and dressings – the red and

Figure 19   Frans Hogenberg, Prince of Orange and Burgomaster Van Stralen attempting to pacify a Calvinist crowd near the Meirbrug, *engraving, 21 × 28 cm. Note the large number of timber houses still in evidence (14 March 1587). Copyright Museum Plantin-Moretus/Print Room, Antwerp III/H.70/6.*

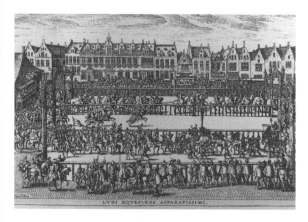

Figure 20   Pieter van der Borcht, Ludi Equestres Appartissimi, *jousting in Roman costume on the Meir, engraving, from J. Bochius,* Descriptio publicae gratulationis, *1595, Antwerp, Moretus. Copyright Museum Plantin-Moretus/Print Room, Antwerp III/R.45.1.*

white style known as 'streaky bacon' (**Pl. 29**, p.40). Most of the houses had large multi-storeyed attics for storage, with a crane beam and loading door prominent in the elevations. There were also huge cellars, which in places were joined up to make a system of underground streets. You can see the large loading doors for these cellars in the Boloniensis map and in Fig. 21. Storage is the key to wealth in trading communities, and some goods would circulate from owner to owner as fortunes changed and cargo manifests filled and emptied.

The ceremonial centre of Antwerp was the Grote Markt. Originally the markets and fairs were held here, but soon these were moved further out to the Meir (**Col. Pl. 5**, p.118). The

Figure 21 Hendrik Causé, Old town hall Antwerp, *engraving, 32 × 34 cm, after a painting by G. Mostaert, c.1560, from* Album Linnig II, *p.67, Antwerp Printenkabinett. Copyright Museum Plantin-Moretus/Print Room, Antwerp.*

Meir could also be used for popular festivals such as the Ommegangen and special events (Fig. 20). The old Stadhuis or town hall was a picturesque Gothic affair (Fig. 21). Notice the lean-to shelter where the magistrates could do business seated at benches. On this engraving the line of the foundations of the new Stadhuis are marked out. Completed in 1567, it was an imposing affair dressed in stone and in an Italian Renaissance style (see **Pls 30, 31**, p.41). The architect seems to have been Cornelis de Vriendt, who also built several town houses in the city (see **Pl. 62**, p.61). During the same period, many of the wooden guild and merchants' houses lining the Grote Markt were rebuilt in brick and stone (see **Pl. 52**, p.54). A great deal of rebuilding and restoration has changed the appearance in detail of these buildings, but the general effect matches the views we have in engravings.

The commercial centre of Antwerp was the Beurs or Exchange. The first Beurs, dating from 1485, has disappeared without trace but was little more than a standard wooden merchant's house with a courtyard and cloister. In 1515 Domien de Waghemakere was commissioned to pull down the old wooden building and erect a new 'House of the Great Rhine' to serve as an Exchange. Sections of arcading from the second Beurs have survived (**Pl. 32**, p.42). The house has been completely rebuilt, but the tower remains in the corner (**Pl. 33**, p.42). One of the towers along J2–J3 (middle) shows where it was. The cusped arches are of the late Gothic kind typical of this architect's work and similar to the arcade in the Hof Van Lieere (**Pl. 34**, p.42).

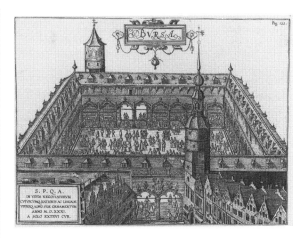

Figure 22 Pieter van der Borcht, New Exchange or Handelsbeurs, *c.1532, engraving, 23.5 × 31.5 cm, from Lodovico Guiccardini,* Descrittioni di tutti i Paesi Bassi, *Plantin, 1581. Copyright Museum Plantin-Moretus/Print Room, Antwerp III/B.337.*

Figure 23 Pieter van der Borcht, Hansa house, *c.1564, engraving, 23.7 × 31.5 cm, from Lodovico Guiccardini,* Descrittioni di tutti i Paesi Bassi, *Plantin, 1581. Copyright Museum Plantin-Moretus/Print Room, Antwerp III/B.337.*

A new Beurs was commissioned in 1526–7 and completed by 1531 (Fig. 22). You can identify it easily on the Boloniensis since it occupies a complete city block (H4) with a new street giving access to the centre of each side.

Nothing remains of the English Exchange, nor of the very large Hansa house built at around the same time as the Stadhuis to provide storage and accommodation to the German nation (Fig. 23). It was built in the Nieuwstad (O3) and provided with a tall tower (not shown on the Boloniensis). The canals on either side were wide and deep enough for ocean-going ships to dock directly. Another building in the Nieuwstad built in 1563–6 to accommodate the North German trades was the Coophuys or Hessenhuis (Pl. 35, p.43). It became a centre for the German soldiers in the imperial army, serving as barracks and Lutheran chapel as well as store house (Pl. 36, p.43). The high arches allowed the hooped wagons characteristic of the overland trade to Germany to enter.

4 STABILITY AND INSTABILITY: A COMPARATIVE ANALYSIS

DAVID ENGLANDER

'It is notorious that Antwerp was but yesterday the first and principal ornament of all Europe, the refuge of all the nations of the world, the nurse of all arts and industries; … the protector of the Roman Catholic religion, she was ever faithful and obedient to her sovereign prince and lord. The city is now changed to a gloomy cavern, filled with robbers and murderers, enemies to God, to the king, and to all good subjects.' So wrote the estates of Brabant on the morrow of the Spanish Fury, the bloody three days in November 1576 when Philip II's unpaid and undisciplined troops ran amok, destroying persons and property in what, until then, had been one of the finest cities in all Christendom. What brought them to Antwerp? The answer is religion. Antwerp was caught up in the maelstrom unleashed by the Reformation. The shock waves were more than the city could bear. Confessional conflict directly and indirectly brought Antwerp's Golden Age to a close.

Its absence from Venice is striking, all the more so since contemporaries were convinced that nowhere was more likely to be laid low by religion than the Serene Republic. God's wrath,

visited upon its refractory rulers and compliant citizens, was periodically predicted. Crusades against Venice were frequently deemed no less – and sometimes more – desirable than those against the Turk. Not that the maritime republic, for all its oriental magnificence, harboured heresy or infidelity, at least not beyond the necessities of trade. What so irked the faithful was its curious **Erastianism** in ecclesiastical affairs combined with its unswerving orthodoxy in matters of personal belief. 'The great piety of the Venetians, to which their numerous churches still bear silent witness,' wrote the author of an approved *History of the Popes,* 'seems to contrast strangely with these efforts to subjugate the Church to the State.' The Venetians nevertheless appear to have struck the right balance between the secular and the spiritual. Venice, unlike Antwerp, never became a centre for heresy and sedition: religion in general remained a source of integration rather than subversion. Venice eventually succumbed to the godless armies of Napoleon two centuries after Antwerp's submission to the Catholic contingents of Philip II. By the time of Farnese's reconquest, the basis of Antwerp's primacy in the European world economy had been undermined. The question, therefore, naturally arises: why was religion so destructive a force in Antwerp, or, to put it another way, why were the Venetians better able to manage the conflicts of the age than their counterparts in Antwerp?

To tackle this question I propose to look first at the potential causes of unrest and the possible sources of religious pluralism and then analyse the factors for stability in both cities.

4.1 FOREIGN COMMUNITIES

A potent condition for dissent was the presence in both cities of large numbers of foreign merchants. 'Here' on Piazza San Marco, wrote a wide-eyed and open-mouthed Englishman, 'you may see all manner of fashions of attire, and heare all the languages of Christendome, besides those that are spoken by the barbarous Ethnickes.' The babble of foreign tongues was, indeed, overwhelming. Besides the Spanish, Portuguese, French, German and English merchants who thronged the Rialto, the business district was crowded with Armenians, Cypriots, Maronites, Syrians, Georgians, Moors, Persians, Jews and long-haired Greeks who, according to our English visitor, were 'fustian, unseemly and very ruffian-like'. Antwerp was no less welcoming. Above the New Exchange of 1531 was inscribed a celebration of the merchants 'of all nations and tongues' whose presence made the city the commercial capital of the world. Their numbers were considerable. In mid-sixteenth-century Antwerp the number of men in the foreign community represented about 5 per cent of the total adult male population, a figure unsurpassed in any town of the Western world at that time.

Their presence entailed adjustments in matters of faith. Protestants who did not cause scandal were, in general, allowed to profess their religion in private. Turks, too, were so privileged. Greeks in Venice were numbered among the faithful. The fiction that the Greek Orthodox Church was merely a variant form of Catholicism enabled public worship to proceed at San Georgio dei Greci, the focal point of the 3,000 strong expatriate community. Jews were different.

While all minority groups were subject to close regulation and surveillance, Jews alone suffered discrimination on grounds of religion. Restrictions were imposed on the work they performed, where they lived, even the clothes they wore. You will find more on this in Section 10.

From the fourteenth century (earlier in the case of the Serenissima) Jews had maintained a precarious presence in both Venice and Antwerp. By the sixteenth century Venetian Jewry was easily the larger of the two communities. Recruited from German, Italian, Levantine and Iberian merchants, it numbered some 1,694 persons in 1586. Antwerp Jewry, by contrast, numbered fewer than 400 people, who were drawn almost exclusively from Portuguese New Christians or **Marranos**. New Christians who reverted to their old faith were deemed to be heretics and treated accordingly. The Portuguese New Christians who dispersed to Antwerp and Venice, following the forcible conversions of 1497, were the object of considerable suspicion. Orders for their expulsion from Venice and its dominions were issued in 1497 and renewed in 1550. But whereas Portuguese Marranos constituted one among the Jewish 'nations' of Venice, Antwerp Jewry was almost totally Marrano in make-up. An adequate history of this covert community has yet to be written. But if its internal life remains opaque, its outward insecurities are easily documented for Charles V, like the governing élite of Venice, wavered between repression and reconciliation in his policy

towards the Marranos. For reasons of trade they were welcomed at Antwerp; for reasons of state they were sent away. For the city fathers, however, the former outweighed the latter. The emperor's ordinances were, in consequence, 'systematically ignored'. Notwithstanding the antagonism of the imperial inquisition, Portuguese Marranos continued to settle in the city and practise in secret the faith of their fathers.

4.2 IMMIGRATION

Venice and Antwerp, like most towns and cities of the sixteenth century, were unable to maintain adequate population growth and relied upon extensive immigration to sustain production and consumption. Natural increase accounted for a very tiny proportion of urban population growth in this period. Antwerp's population explosion – between 1526 and 1560 it increased from 55,000 to between 90,000 and 100,000 – was due primarily to the influx of people from within the Low Countries and from as far afield as France, Italy and the Iberian peninsula. Christopher Plantin, whose publishing-printing establishment at Antwerp was one of the wonders of the age, was a Frenchman. Similarly, the founder of the Aldine Press was not a native of Venice but from Crete. Most immigrants, though, were destined for neither fame nor fortune.

What brought them to the city? Some came in search of work, some came in search of a spouse, and some came in search of food and shelter. War and famine periodically sent the rural poor scurrying townwards in search of relief. Marino Sanuto, the great Venetian diarist, noted the mass of homeless beggars and displaced persons who roamed the city streets and lodged beneath the porticos in the winter of 1527–8. 'Apart from the poor who belong to Venice and are crying in the streets,' he remarked, 'they have come from the island of Burano, mostly with their clothes upon their heads and children in their arms, asking for charity. And many have come from the provinces of Vicenza and Brescia – a shocking thing.' Some like the rogues, vagabonds and beggars from Padua, Morghera and other regions were seasonal visitors; others moved with the job. Bakers' journeymen, said a report of 1611, 'are all northerners, Germans and outsiders who don't care where they are'. In sixteenth-century Venice deficiencies in labour supply were exceptional. Shortages created by the plague of 1576–7, which wiped out between one-quarter and one-third of the city's inhabitants, were made good with extraordinary rapidity; within ten years the population had virtually recovered its pre-plague level.

Antwerp, too, seems to have experienced little difficulty in satisfying its labour requirements. As with Venice, death and disease and displacement due to war were important agents in the transfer of people from the countryside to the town. Not all, though, were distressed or desperate folk. Analysis of the origins and occupations of the 768 heads of families who migrated from the bishopric of Liège between 1533 and 1600 suggests that newcomers to Antwerp were not simply country yokels up from the farm, but included substantial numbers of craftsmen and clothworkers, bakers, tailors, tanners, merchants and men of modest means; 16 per cent were townsmen from Liège itself. Their motives were mixed. Some were 'pushed' by the decline of their trades, others 'pulled' by the superior wage-rates and placements within the Antwerp labour market.

4.3 SOCIAL STRUCTURE

The world they had entered differed markedly from that of the villages and communes in which they had grown up. The sheer pressure of numbers affected spatial, social and productive relations. Expression of social divisions in terms of three estates – clergy, nobility and the rest – became increasingly problematic even in Venice, which possessed a social framework that was more formal and less dynamic than its thrusting rival in the north. The social structure of Venice was divided into a set of formally defined status groups, each with its own privileges, and also included numerous corporations with specific obligations and rights specializing in particular spheres of social and economic action. Antwerp, the great boom town of the sixteenth century, was socially more fluid than Venice, but nevertheless retained much that was traditional in its forms of social and economic organization. Trades guilds and devotional confraternities, the Church and the magistrature – such were the principal means by which conflict could be contained, piety promoted and property preserved, for in both cities extremes of wealth and poverty pitted rich against poor. In Venice, as in Antwerp, those who wielded political and economic power confronted a mass of poor and property-less people whose willingness to accept their condition could not be taken for granted.

4.4 SOCIAL UNREST

But whereas sixteenth-century Venice was renowned for its harmonious class relations, Antwerp's reputation for ungovernability grew as the century wore on. That reputation, sustained by the memory of the rebellion of 1477 when the commons rose against prince and magistrature, was kept alive by spasmodic bouts of religious and civil unrest during the years that followed. The city fathers, naturally enough, were keen to downplay its disorderly character – after all, turbulence was not good for trade. Not so Ludovico Guicciardini, whose *Description of the Low Countries*, first published in 1567 and much reprinted thereafter, presents an otherwise flattering portrait of Antwerp at its zenith. Indeed, he specifically denied that the populace had lived down its reputation for riotous and seditious conduct towards the magistrates and lords of the city. In support of this contention he cited the rising of 1477 and the beer riots of 1554 which, in his view, constituted one of the three remarkable happenings of modern times. In this he was not alone. The ugly mood of the populace was also noted by the Venetian ambassador who, in a dispatch to the magistracy written shortly afterwards, offered the opinion that fresh attempts by the authorities to raise direct taxation so as to satisfy the emperor's cash requirements, 'as they did lately, would to my knowledge hazard a fresh insurrection, the people having rebelled on this account at Antwerp, and other places'. The same perception was, indeed, shared by the emperor himself. The decision to build a citadel to the south of the town, taken by Charles V but executed by his son Philip II, was partly a response to the beer riots of 1539 and the social unrest that prevailed.

The source of that unrest was in large part economic. Whatever their varying relation to prices, wages in the sixteenth century were not sufficient to support a family. For those in regular employment, living standards were low. For those who occupied an inferior position in the labour market, life was unbearably hard. In both Antwerp and Venice there existed a large pool of unincorporated labour living a hand-to-mouth existence as unskilled day labourers. 'They were the equivalent of the nineteenth-century lumpen proletariat, owning no property, unable to buy themselves into a guild and obliged to subsist on low wages from casual work,' writes Leon Voet (1973), Antwerp's historian. 'They were an anonymous mass whose numbers cannot even be guessed; a suppressed and submissive part of the population of whom nothing was heard in normal circumstances, and who only in times of prolonged economic malaise and grain shortages demonstrated on the streets and broke a few windows.' The republic, too, had to contend with a reserve army of labour which was equally troublesome and dangerous.

4.5 IMPACT OF THE REFORMATION

In both cities the presence of so many foreigners of different faiths and practices increased the disruptive potential generated by urbanism and **capitalism**. Here we merely need note that their presence helped to sharpen the Reformation crisis. Indeed, Catholic critics were convinced that these outsiders were the cause of the crisis. Bishop Granvelle, Philip II's advisor on the Low Countries, thought that it was the evangelical reformers among Antwerp's foreign merchant communities who had fomented rebellion among the locals and 'turned them into dangerous men, preaching freedom to them and blinding them with a belief in their own greatness and that they did not have to accept being governed but should seek to govern themselves'. Protestant merchants were also thought to occupy a pivotal role in the growth of heresy in Venice.

By comparison with Antwerp, however, the Reformation in Venice was very small beer indeed. Almost from the beginning of the break with Rome, the city on the Scheldt was a hotbed of heresy. 'Antwerp', writes Cornelius Krahn (1936), 'was one of the first and chief centres for spreading the influence of the Reformation in the Low Countries.' Luther's writings had reached the city by 1518 and were being reprinted by 1520. Of the 129 editions of Luther's works published in the Low Countries from 1521 to 1541, 85, possibly 90, were published in Antwerp. Protestantism, moreover, was popular. When, in 1585, the city was finally conquered for Catholicism, some 40,000 dissidents departed. These **nonconformists** – Lutherans and Anabaptists but mainly Calvinists – were drawn largely from shopkeepers, artisans and the labouring poor. These were the people who joined secret conventicles, supplied armed support for the hedge preachers, undertook prison breaks, intimidated the magistrates and encouraged the **iconoclasm** that swept through the Low Countries in the 'Wonderyear' of 1566. Without them the process of Calvinization in the government, administration and defence of

the city (1577–85) could not have succeeded. But they were not alone, for Protestantism in the Low Countries was more than a movement from below. To the Netherlandish nobility and urban bourgeoisie the Reformation supplied an ideology for the defence of local and class privilege against a centralizing monarch which finally found fruition in the rise of the Dutch Republic. But here the emphasis is upon plebian Protestantism, upon the simple folk who made up the rank and file of the Reformation in Antwerp. What made them tick? Alas, all too little is still known of their innermost thoughts and feelings. But there does appear to be a close connection between religious innovation and social criticism. The hedge preaching did contain elements of class hatred, and it seems unlikely that Calvinism could have secured such popularity without addressing the material condition of the masses.

4.6 SOCIAL INEQUALITY AND RELIGIOUS RADICALISM

Even in Venice, where conditions for the development of a comparable mass movement did not exist, religious radicalism often went hand in glove with an acute awareness of social inequality. The records of the Venetian Inquisition allow us to reconstruct some attitudes and beliefs of the popular classes, to enter the taverns and workshops and observe the intense religious discussions that absorbed the artisan heretics of that city. Two points are noteworthy. First, there was no necessary antagonism between popular culture and literate culture. The cobblers, tailors, printers, jewellers, etc. were avid readers; and since books were often read aloud, illiteracy was no bar to participation. Second, their religion did not occupy a separate sphere but informed their everyday concerns and general outlook. Thus, the unequal distribution of wealth was not merely unjust; it was sinful. 'God', said the silk-weaver Girolamo da Luca, 'has not made one higher than another.' Battista Amai, an itinerant **mercer** and enameller who plied his trade in the Rialto, agreed. 'Our lords are dogs!' he declared, 'cardinals have 40,000 to 50,000 ducats of income; they keep mules, dogs, whores; and they do not give alms as they should. The heretics are better, more charitable, because they love one another, and keep things in common.' Both the shop and the tavern provided a locus for the exchange of ideas, a private space secure from the prying eyes of prince and prelate. The penetration of this space was for those in authority a constant concern. Political propaganda aside, they knew full well that Venetian social stability was not a gift from God but something that had to be worked at; and in Venice, as in Antwerp, maintenance was a full-time occupation.

We have seen that many of the conditions of life in Venice and Antwerp were potentially unstable. But there were compensating factors. The cities possessed resources for self-renewal and change. We will now look at these.

4.7 INDUSTRIAL PRODUCTION

All towns are by definition centres of exchange and distribution, but few sixteenth-century cities combined commercial, financial and industrial functions on a local, regional and international scale as Venice and Antwerp. The division of labour reflected their exceptional character. In addition to the relatively unspecialized craft workers and trades people who made and marketed their own products, there was considerable large- and small-scale industry. Venice was remarkable for her ability to adapt to her loss of eastern markets. A ready market and labour force from her new land empire and the opening up of new trade routes enabled her to expand domestic industrial production. 'Of all sixteenth-century European manufactured goods', writes the economic historian R.T. Rapp (1976), 'only a few were made in a way that could be called "industrial" in the modern sense – employing considerable capital equipment, factory-type production, and division of labour. Naval construction, textile manufacture, glassmaking, and some chemical and metallurgical industries could qualify. Venice was a world leader in every one.'

The production of quality woollen fabrics in which the Venetians traditionally excelled rocketed from an estimated annual output of 2,000 pieces of cloth in the early 1500s to something more than 20,000 pieces during the last third of the century. Indeed, the extra-ordinary expansion of woollen manufacture quite transformed the occupational order; by 1540 it was officially deemed to be 'one of the chief employments of the Venetian people, and a very great livelihood for the poor'. The growth of silk production was no less impressive: between 1493 and 1554 the numbers engaged in silk weaving rose from 500 to 1,200, and by the close of the century it was one of the largest and most profitable industries with upwards of 2,000 looms and 2,000 workers. The Venetians also maintained a

presence in cotton, linen, fustian and canvas-making. In glassware and mirror manufacture Venice was supreme. The products of the Murano glassworks were renowned for their quality, versatility and distinctive coloration, as indeed were many of the luxury items which formed the staple of her world-wide export trade. The scarlets and crimsons which made Venetian fabrics sought after by the world's wealthy were among the varied output of the city's chemical industry which, in addition to processed dyestuffs, produced paints, soaps and other chemicals for sale overseas. Cargoes carried by Venetian galleys also included sugar from the city's refineries and the products of her lace, leatherware, candle-making and jewellery industries.

Antwerp's prosperity, like that of Venice, was sustained by its luxury export industries. Its 'sugar bakers', concentrated along the area of the Werf on the aptly named Suikerrui, processed raw cane from Spain and Portugal for export to England, Germany and France. The Iberian peninsula also supplied the precious stones which, having been turned, cut and polished by the city's expert and highly skilled craftsmen, were sent abroad to the great profit of all. The production of works of art and of musical instruments was another speciality in which Antwerp excelled. Much of the extraordinary output of the city's painters and sculptors was for consumption overseas; innumerable lutes, zithers and clavicymbals produced in local workshops were likewise designed to please foreign ears. Foreign eyes, too, feasted upon the rich, intricate and world-famous tapestries that were woven by Antwerp's export-oriented craft workers. Goldsmiths, silversmiths and craftsmen engaged in clothing, furniture, chests, iron and copperware were equally keen participants in overseas trade. The ability of both cities to convert wealth derived from commerce into exportable goods was an important factor for survival.

But in Venice, as in Antwerp, the urban economy was peculiarly vulnerable to the vagaries of international trade. In both cities the level of economic activity was dependent upon the stability and buoyancy of export markets which, although vastly more profitable than domestic markets, were also more unstable and more easily disrupted. Such over-commitment could yield fabulous returns when trade was good, but mass unemployment when conditions were disturbed. In such circumstances heresy and unbelief might secure a boldness and a mass base which they might otherwise have not possessed. Internal instability, where unmanageable, might also invite outside intervention. Neither Venice nor Antwerp was a free agent in matters of faith; any want of resolve in crushing heresy and subversion could bring forth a visitation from the terrible *tercios* of His Most Catholic Majesty, the King of Spain. From the accession of Philip II (1559), the spectre of Spanish intervention haunted the patriciate in both cities. Their fears were not groundless, for it was a crisis of the kind outlined above which initiated the iconoclasm of 1566–7 and the set of events that brought about the ruination of Antwerp.

Notwithstanding Contarini's panegyrics on her extraordinary social stability, Venice experienced riots in 1569–70 when, according to an eyewitness account, 'people crazy with hunger wandered through the city looking for baker's shops as if they were going to churches to obtain pardons and indulgence'; in 1581 when the Arsenal workers erupted in support of better pay; and again in 1601 when the currency collapsed and bakers declined payment in debased coinage. Antwerp was even more unruly. Beer riots, grain riots, tax riots, wage riots, religious riots – Antwerp suffered the lot. Her turbulent population seemed ever ready to spill on to the streets in order to ventilate their grievances against engrossers, hoarders, speculators and other offenders against customs in common. The arrest of the prior of the Austin Friars in September 1522 on charges of heresy, for example, provoked the populace, who disliked the manner of the proceedings. 'When the Margrave had obtained custody of him by subtle means, he led him to an abbey of White Monks, called St Michael's, where he was to remain till called for,' ran one firsthand account. 'Being a holiday, great numbers of women were there for devotion, and hearing that the Friar was taken, and in the abbey, they broke doors and windows, and compelled his delivery.' Social unrest was sustained by conflict in the workplace. The journeymen clothworkers, who struck when supplies of noncorporate labour were exhausted and masters weak, gave particular cause for concern. To enforce their claims, these strikers formed clandestine combinations which organized demonstrations, flyposted the town, visited resistant workshops, and generally sought to spread sedition throughout the trade. Stroppy printers, organized in autonomous chapels, were equally difficult. Plantin complained of 'the carelessness, drunkenness and malice of my workers' in

1571 and locked them out in 1572. (For other examples see *KMB*, pp.41–4.)

Alarming though they were, the traditional character of these disturbances was, however, understood. Sixteenth-century crowds were not in general moved by political considerations. In the main, they sought the redress of specific grievances rather than the transformation of property relations. The urban patriciate, though it inflicted severe sentences upon alleged ringleaders, perceived the need for a less sanguine engagement in what in effect was a process of bargaining by riot. The increased excise on beer which had provoked the Antwerp riots of 1539 was thus removed once order had been restored. Similarly, the city fathers, notwithstanding support for the masters, deemed it impolitic to resist demands for improved wages following the great clothworkers' strike of 1573–4. The surest method of preventing disorder, however, was to safeguard both the supply and quality of bread, and in Venice, as in Antwerp, magisterial interventions were frequent on both counts. The large granaries in Venice bore witness to this commitment (Map 1). Coercion, we may therefore conclude, was a necessary but not a sufficient condition of social stability. Other instruments were available for the reconciliation of rich and poor. Chief amongst them were the trade guilds and devotional confraternities, whose role in the preservation of orthodoxy and order we shall soon consider.

4.8 ARISTOCRACIES

We have seen that both cities were governed by aristocracies. How did the ruling classes in both cities adapt to internal and external pressures? The process of élite recruitment was broadly similar. In Venice, as in Antwerp, family connection, patronage and wealth mattered. In spite of their contrasting structures – open in Antwerp and closed in Venice – both patriciates displayed a high level of endogamy in each patriciate and in the considerable support given to patricians by their close kin as guardians, executors and godparents. Financial support, too, was often forthcoming, certainly in the case of Venice, be it for the payments of dowries or as assistance to patricians in trading difficulties. Marriage and kinship, in short, were the most important links within each patriciate.

The extensive kinship network which linked these families gave the patriciate homogeneity and continuity. These families controlled but never monopolized the major sources of wealth in the urban economy – long-distance trade and landownership. But whereas the Venetian patriciate was a commercially minded aristocracy that increasingly preferred the pursuit of pleasure to the pursuit of money, the rulers of Antwerp were never anything more than commercially minded landowners with property in both town and country. Thus Antoon van Stralen, four times burgomaster since 1555, though not himself a merchant – his wealth came from the real estate business – lent money to the high and mighty and was no stranger to the Beurs. These men, aptly described by the English as 'the lords of Antwerp', though they hobnobbed with the Netherlandish nobility and did not themselves engage in trade, were sensitive to its requirements. Their situation was thus unlike that of the rulers of the maritime republic whose wealth, in spite of the trappings of gentility, had originated in merchandise and movable goods. Variations in the composition of patrician incomes indeed suggests contrasts in the life-style of the two élites.

Most striking was the transformation effected in the style of life of the Venetian patriciate. The gradual decline of long-distance trade as a source of patrician income, together with the proportionate increase in the influence of land and house property, accompanied a redefinition of relations with the mainland. The economic penetration of the terra firma, which has been variously explained, represented a process of adjustment to the loss of traditional markets. It was partly a reaction to the expansion of Turkish power in the Levant and eastern Mediterranean, partly a response to the Portuguese discoveries of the new route to the Indies, and partly conditioned by a growing need to secure self-sufficiency in the supply of food. The shock of the battle of Agnadello in 1509 may also have served to concentrate attention and capital on the mainland. Whatever the reason or precise combination of reasons, there is no denying the patrician presence on the terra firma. The magnificent palazzi that lined the Grand Canal came increasingly to complement the equally grand structures that rose up on the mainland estates. 'Of the 1,400 mainland villas in Venetian territory that are classed as of artistic interest,' writes F.C. Lane (1973), '15 were built in the fourteenth century, 84 in the fifteenth, and over 250 in the sixteenth century.'

About the disposition and investments of the Antwerp patriciate we are rather less well informed. Its position was not strictly comparable with that of Venice simply because, unlike Venice and its terra firma, Antwerp's relations with its hinterland were market-led rather than imposed by force of arms. All that we can say is that whatever changes in outlook and investment occurred during the sixteenth century, there is no evidence to suggest that the urban orientation of Antwerp's city fathers was affected thereby.

In Antwerp, as in Venice, government was essentially oligarchical in character. In both cities, too, the ruling élite was recruited from an inner group of patrician families. 'The lists of burgomasters and other officials indicate how the same families supplied municipal rulers not merely for generations but for centuries,' writes G.D. Ramsay (1975). 'The van der Werve, who were prominent in the thirteenth century, were still supplying burgomasters in the second half of the sixteenth.' The extent of oligarchical control of civil life also supplies an opportunity to compare and contrast forms of urban government and the degree of autonomy which each city enjoyed.

It wasn't the case that the city was free of all external interference, however. From the Royal Palace in Brussels the regent and her council kept a close watch on affairs during the prolonged absence of the sovereign. Periodic payments – in the form of taxes, subsidies and other capital transfers – were also required by a debt-ridden prince whose untoward interventions in financial markets – the Spanish government thrice defaulted – had likewise to be borne patiently. For all that, the 'lords of Antwerp' enjoyed a very considerable latitude in the management of affairs, even to the extent of negotiating foreign treaties on their own authority. Antwerp, declared Guicciardini, 'rules and governs itself, as if autonomous, almost like a free city and Republic'. SPQA, that audacious emblem of which the city fathers were inordinately fond, was as much republican as Roman in character. Attempts at centralization were resisted by a noncompliant magistrature which displayed remarkable tenacity in defence of the liberties and privileges of the city. Charles V's repeated attempts to regulate the religious life of the city through the introduction of a lay inquisition was frustrated by a patriciate which believed that bigotry was bad for trade and a denial of the citizen's customary right to trial in a local court. The city fathers did not, however, contemplate any general extension of religious rights, and with good reason. Toleration that exceeded trade requirements was in the eyes of the emperor and his son a dangerous form of heresy to be extirpated by force if need be. The magistrates, good Catholics to a man, would not willingly provoke their prince.

Circumspection in confessional conflict was by no means a Brabantine peculiarity; the Venetians were equally restricted in their freedom of action. Notwithstanding differences in status, both were constrained by the hegemony of the **Habsburgs**. Agnadello was to Venice what Alva was to Antwerp – that is, a brutal exposure of the limitations of power. The magistracy, no less than their Brabantine compeers, lived in fear of Philip II and his father. In the eyes of Catholic critics Venice was vulnerable to heretical ideas. Her willingness to tolerate heterodox foreigners from Greek Orthodox communicants to German Protestant merchants, coupled with her traditional antagonism towards the Holy See, cast her as the conduit for carrying the Reformation into Italy. Although these fears were without foundation, it was deemed impolitic to reject papal pressure for firm measures against the enemies of God. Unable to resist the introduction of the Roman Inquisition, the Venetians sought by stealth to protect their trade and territory from the pontiff's people. Three lay magistrates, appointed to assist the Venetian Inquisition, served to moderate its proceedings and uphold the state's vital interests. Curial critics, who continued to cavil and carp, tended, however, to confuse tolerance with intransigence. Venice's nondogmatic attitude in matters of faith, which so infuriated the votaries of orthodoxy, was not a denial of the Catholic communion. Such a denial, in the view of one eminent scholar, would not only have affronted the mass of Venetians but 'exposed Venice to attack, and probable absorption by Spain'.

In summary, neither the Venetian nor the Antwerp patriciate was 'soft' on heresy. In both cities religious dissidence was perceived as a threat to degree, priority and place, and dealt with accordingly.

4.9 GUILDS

Below the level of the ruling patriciate, the guilds played a key role in maintaining stability. Trades guilds, we noted earlier (Block I, Section 7), discharged economic, religious and confraternal duties. Here we are concerned with their role as agents of integration. These associations, which incorporated two-thirds of the Venetian labour force and the greater portion of the craft workers and retailers of Antwerp, came in all shapes and sizes. There were guilds of small producers and guilds of industrial magnates, guilds of merchants and guilds of retailers. Some were federations of allied trades, others occupationally specific. Most were male-dominated but not all. The *appelwijven* ('apple wives') of Antwerp had their separate corporation, while the Venetian guild structure reserved space for female metalworkers and mercers as well as women workers in the textile and clothing trades. The multiplicity of guilds – there were upwards of 100 in Antwerp and as many in Venice – and their distinctive characteristics were in part historically determined, but also reflected the differing degrees of specialization in the various trades. In those trades in which division of labour was minimal, the guild embraced the entire workforce; where the production process necessitated a more extensive division of labour, guilds organized the workers in each separate process.

Guilds in Venice and Antwerp were subject to a high degree of civic regulation. Their governing statutes, formalized in writing since the thirteenth century, were available for inspection and revision by the authorities. These rules and regulations generally defined the degree of self-government which each guild possessed in relation to the election of officers, trade jurisdiction and miscellaneous professional and public duties which they were expected to perform. The latter were considerable, for sixteenth-century guilds were something more than mere private associations preoccupied with trade and technical matters. Guilds supplied the means whereby resources might be mobilized for internal and external defence as well as for purposes of public display and ceremonial. Antwerp had its specialized military guilds who in times of civil commotion were required to put the burgher on the beat, while from 1539 onwards Venetian guilds bore a general responsibility to supply oarsmen for the galleys. Naval defence, with its insatiable demands for cash and conscripts, transformed the Venetian guild system into a quasi-official tax and man-gathering agency. In other ways, too, guilds were closely involved in the process of government. Measures to prevent the sale of food unfit for human consumption were, for example, enforced partly by public health officials and partly by the guilds. In short, the guilds were too important to be left to the guildsmen.

The authorities not only determined the status and functions of the guilds but also supervised their activities. Deans of the various guilds were appointed annually by Antwerp magistrates, who also settled demarcation disputes and intra-guild conflicts. Charters for new corporations, alterations to statutes and changes in registration fees likewise required external approval. Recalcitrant guilds were punished severely. The cloth dyers' guild, for example, which fell foul of the magistrates in connection with the enforcement of certain quality control measures, was opened – in effect dissolved – in 1583 and remained so for fourteen years. Venetian magistrates possessed a comparable authority; as in Antwerp, guild officers had to be acceptable to the magistrates. The authorities in Venice also deployed an army of inspectors and informers to maintain standards and monitor performance.

In both cities, then, government was represented in the guilds, but only in Antwerp were the guilds represented in government. Labour in Venice was rigidly excluded from any form of political power by the magistracy. In Antwerp members of the guilds had a voice in the deliberations of the Monday Council, an advisory committee which reviewed guild and market regulations, and in the Broad Council, which determined taxation. On both councils, though, access was restricted to a privileged minority of guilds whose deans alone were eligible for membership. These dilute forms of representation were but a shadow of the power-sharing arrangements wrested from the patriciate during the *Quaey Wereld* ('Evil World'), the guild-led uprising of 1477 which opened the college of magistrates to the commons. It was a temporary triumph. Popular fury, though directed at the magistrates, provoked the intervention of an irate prince – in this case Maximilian of Habsburg, the future emperor – who saw subversion and anarchy as the only outcome. The rebellion was crushed, the gains nullified, and the *status quo ante* restored. It all took time but by 1487 'the commons were again shut out of municipal life'.

The absence of effective political participation does not, however, mean that order was simply a matter of coercion and control imposed from above upon an unwilling workforce. On the contrary. In both Venice and Antwerp trade regulations were often the product of initiatives that were brought from the guilds to the magistrates for approval. Communication between the authorities and the guilds was, in fact, constant. Venetian

guilds also enjoyed a right of petition for the presentation of demands and redress of grievances. 'These procedures were invoked continuously and the records of the government indicate a high degree of responsiveness,' writes one authority. 'The very fact that there is no incidence of any major upheaval by workers', he concluded, 'suggests that this system of government by appeal was successful.' The initiative did not always come from below. The authorities themselves often sought actively to secure corporate co-operation and consent in maintaining the social order. The Antwerp magistrates, for example, did not hesitate to invoke guild support via the Broad Council in order to sustain its campaign against heresy. The Broad Council that assembled at the close of July 1525 was summoned simply to furnish a mandate for the execution of a popular Protestant preacher. In short, social stability represented a process of negotiation rather than imposition. The authorities in both cities could not snap their fingers, bark an order, and expect compliance. Patrician power could not be sustained by force of arms alone. Trade guilds and confraternities, the essential intermediaries between rulers and ruled, exacted a price for their support of the civic order.

EXERCISE

Guilds and confraternities provided piety and philanthropy and more. Contarini's analysis of the five *Scuole Grandi* (*Anthology* II.1) suggests additional political and social roles. What are they? Re-read *Anthology* II.1 now.

DISCUSSION

Trades guilds and devotional confraternities are clearly presented here as an important instrument of social control. These institutions, Contarini observes, provided the members with something more than mutual aid and spiritual succour; they also supplied an alternative hierarchy within which ambitions for office and honour could be satisfied. Scholars, contemporary and modern, are agreed that political and social stability owed much to the opportunities for rank and recognition created by the guilds and confraternities of sixteenth-century Venice. Contarini's argument, baldly summarized, is that the pursuit of prestige within a controlled corporate environment compensated the disfranchised masses for the absence of political power. Himself a nobleman, Contarini presents these pursuits as a testament to the skill and sagacity of a perspicacious and politically astute patriciate. Historians who might perhaps dispute the Venetian's manipulative interpretation and *de haut en bas* perspective nevertheless concur with his judgement. Brian Pullan (1971), doyen of students of Renaissance Venice, wrote that 'office in the Scuole Grandi did bestow honour and glory and was eagerly sought after' and that 'the Scuole do seem to have offered opportunities for playing politics without disturbing the fabric of the patrician state'. Frederick C. Lane, no less eminent an authority, is equally emphatic. The guilds, he wrote, 'provided opportunities for craftsmen and shopkeepers to hold positions of honour among their fellows and, above all, gave them the feeling of having a place in the social life of the city, a sense of belonging' (Lane, 1973). We are rather less well informed about the effects of Antwerp's guilds and confraternities, but there is no reason to believe that, in functional terms, they were very different.

A primary object of the guild system was to prevent the growth of dependent producers within the workforce. In this Antwerp guildsmen were markedly less successful than their Venetian compeers. 'There is no doubt', writes one authority, 'that in the first half of the sixteenth century the gap between rich and poor craftsmen widened.' The process of differentiation, though uneven in distribution, was most pronounced in the building and textile trades, the two growth industries which made extensive use of unskilled and semi-skilled labour. The ratio of journeymen to masters, set at two to one in the early years of the century, was abandoned in 1536 when the cloth finishers' guild agreed that masters could hire eight labourers. This maximum was raised to sixteen in 1554, and to twenty-two in 1556. Similar changes occurred in other branches of the trade. Increasing concentration within the building trades proved no less divisive. Journeymen bricklayers refused guild subscriptions in 1574, and in 1581 were so unruly and intransigent that the dean and treasurer were unable to make the customary annual collection. But while bricklayers withheld their dues, clothworkers withheld their labour. Following the great clothworkers' strike of 1573–4, the masters instituted a leaving certificate in order to tighten labour discipline and prevent the growth of *compagnonnages* (workers' associations) amongst their journeymen.

Industrial disturbance, though not unknown in Venice – the shearmen, for example, organized a successful strike in the wool industry in 1556 – was perhaps less frequent than in Antwerp. No doubt the ferocious punishments meted out to activists served to deter militancy. For having incited his workmates to protest to the authorities about the inadequate wages they received, Antonio de Zuane, an oarmaker at the Arsenal, was condemned to death. But, as we noted earlier, the maintenance of social stability required more than repression. There is in fact some evidence of significant variation in official attitudes towards industrial organization in the two cities. Unlike the Antwerp patriciate, which 'systematically supported' the masters in their attempts to reduce the independence of journeymen, the Venetian magistrature intervened repeatedly to moderate the growth of dependency.

4.10   SUPPRESSION OF HERESY

In Antwerp, as in Venice, there was no modern separation of administrative, judicial and political functions; the magistrature in both cities discharged judicial and executive duties in like manner. Punishments were brutal and martyrs many. In Antwerp alone 161 heretics were executed in the name of God between 1525 and 1566. The vast majority, however, were neither Lutheran nor Calvinist. Of the 103 persons who between 1555 and 1566 were burnt for their beliefs, at least 91 were Anabaptist and only seven Calvinists. Anabaptists, with their communitarian ideas, were evidently perceived as a greater threat to Christendom than either Luther or Calvin, who if they did not respect God at least respected property. Above the Grote Markt, the preferred spot for such burnings, the smoke rose regularly, perhaps too regularly – for so far from deterrence there seemed to be a direct relationship between the number of executions and the growth of heresy. 'As almost every week some one is burnt in the towns of these Provinces,' wrote the Venetian ambassador, 'it is surprising that this fire cannot be quenched, and that it should break out again more and more daily.'

The Venetian Inquisition was, by contrast, an altogether less bloody business. Only two dozen heretics, possibly less, were thus dispatched. The Venetians, moreover, declined to make punishment into a public spectacle. Unwilling to furnish the condemned with an audience of uncertain sympathies, they preferred strangulation in the privacy of the prison cell or discreet drownings after dark. The unruly scenes at the Grote Markt were not reproduced at Piazza San Marco. But then

Venetian Anabaptism, by comparison with Antwerp, was a marginal concern – a mere 35 of the 1,500 cases that came before the inquisition were so classified. These, however, received capital sentences in disproportionately large numbers. The Venetian Inquisition, unlike the authorities in Antwerp, was preoccupied with witches, judaizers and, above all, mainstream Protestantism. Cases of 'Lutheranism' accounted for more than half (53 per cent) of the total number of proceedings that came before it during the second half of the sixteenth century.

The inquisition was as much concerned with the prevention of heresy as with its pursuit and punishment. The Index of prohibited books, promulgated in the Netherlands in 1546 and in Venice three years later, became the principal instrument of preventative supervision. The vetting of unsuitable reading material, though as old as the Church itself, was made pressing by the advent of printing and the impetus it provided to the circulation of heretical ideas. The initiative, though, did not always rest with the clergy. In the Low Countries the system of political and religious censorship, built up in response to the growth of Protestantism in the first half of the sixteenth century, was largely the work of Charles V and Philip II. Notwithstanding its fearful provisions and formidable detail, the censorship was inefficient and easily evaded. Indeed, the greatest exponent of its deficiencies was none other than the king's 'arch typographer' Christopher Plantin, who, though outwardly conforming, was himself a heretic, issuing unlicensed titles anonymously or under a false imprint (as seen in TV 4). Such publications, moreover, did not only disturb continental Catholics. The English Privy Council, for example, was equally alarmed by the 'lewde, seditious bokes from Andwerpe' circulating within the realm. The Venetian authorities, who were no less apprehensive, found suppression equally difficult. As in Antwerp, the censorship confronted a clandestine book trade with an elaborate smuggling network which continued to supply the market for prohibited books until the close of the 1580s.

The inquisition was not, however, the sole instrument of repression that was available to the authorities. Control, social and spiritual, was enforced by the courts – aided by a network of narks and sundry purveyors of police intelligence. Most notable among them were the parish priests who, in Venice, were – somewhat unusually – partly selected by their parishioners. Magisterial surveillance within the city was both extensive and disturbing. Michel de Montaigne (1533–92), the famous French essayist who kept a travel journal of his visit to Venice in 1580, registered the remarks of one foreign diplomat who said that the Venetians 'were such a suspicious sort of people that if one of their gentlemen spoke to him twice, they would hold him suspect'. Antwerp's internal intelligence system was puny by comparison. Not until the Spanish occupation of the 1570s did the authorities equip themselves with a corps of spies and informers – the *zevenstuivers* ('seven stivers'), so called because of the daily rate of remuneration which the authorities allowed.

Should we conclude, therefore, that superior statecraft explains the more disturbed condition of the Antwerp guilds compared with those of Venice? I think not. Our survey of the relations of rulers and ruled suggests that, in spite of numerous similarities, ultimately it is the difference in the situation of the two communities that is so striking. The marginal impact of the Reformation in Venice meant that the magistracy never confronted a conjunctural crisis comparable with that faced by the city fathers in Antwerp. Venice was not turned upside down by the conjoint effects of religious, social and political unrest. The Venetian guilds were not caught up in the radicalizing process which transformed their Antwerp analogues into the leaders of the 'second iconoclasm', a form of craft Calvinism that flared up in the summer of 1581 and resulted in the dismantling of the guild altars in the cathedral of Our Lady. Similarly, Venetian civic ritual remained a source of integration and did not become a vehicle for the propagation of reformed religion as, for example, did the Antwerp Chambers of Rhetoric. This does not mean that Venice was in any sense more secular in outlook. On the contrary. In Venice, as in Antwerp, prayer, penitential processions, votive art, amulets, the cult of saints and relics continued to supply the principal response to war, famine and everyday disasters. Palladio's church of *Il Redentore* (Christ the Redeemer), built to commemorate the end of the plague of 1577, illustrates the point perfectly (see *Illustration Book 2*, TV 6, **Pls 9, 10**, p.18).

PART TWO
PATRONAGE AND OWNERSHIP IN VENICE AND ANTWERP

5 THE GUILDS AND CONFRATERNITIES AND THEIR PATRONAGE

DIANA NORMAN

One apparent difference between the guilds of Venice and Antwerp lay in their members' political status. In Venice the patriciate had exclusive rights over the constitutional institutions of the city whereas the guildsmen were effectively disenfranchised. In Antwerp the privileged guilds (*ambachten*) had certain political prerogatives by virtue of their representation on the Broad and Monday Councils. Nevertheless, the agenda for these legislative councils was controlled by the patrician magistrates. Despite this lack of direct participation in government, the urban patriciate of both cities depended on the trade guilds to maintain social order. The trade guilds acted as essential intermediaries in this process, but as representatives of certain occupational interests they often exacted a price for their co-operation.

Confraternities constituted another important form of civic institution. In the case of Antwerp it is possible to cite a number of instances where the city's guilds overlapped with the confraternities. For example, the guild of soapmakers shared an altar in the cathedral with the confraternity of the Sacrament, and the Violieren Chamber of Rhetoric (attached to the painters' guild of Saint Luke) formed its own religious brotherhood devoted to the cult of the Seven Sorrows of the Virgin. In addition to these guild associations there were several major confraternities in Antwerp: the confraternities of the Holy Cross, the Holy Circumcision, the Holy Sacrament, Praise of Our Lady, *Salve Regina*, Saint Anthony Abbot and Saint Roch. As is clear from their titles, these lay confraternities were formed in order to focus their members' piety upon either a local relic or a specific form of devotion or a therapeutic saint. Apart from these major confraternities, there were also innumerable smaller confraternities. All had a mixed membership of patrician and popular elements.

In Antwerp there were also two other kinds of corporate institution which did not have an equivalent in Venice. First, there were the military guilds or shooting companies (*shuttersgilde*). According to Guicciardini (1567) these comprised six in number: two of *arbalestriers* (crossbowmen), two of archers, one of *arquebusiers* (musketeers) and one of two-hand swordsmen. Each company had its own distinctive costume and regularly took part in the city's civic processions. (**Pl. 37**, p.44 depicts a drummer of the Antwerp guild of archers.) Apart from these ceremonial and military duties, these companies also held festivals and shooting competitions. Pieter Bruegel the Elder provides one record of the kind of rural festivities that took place on the feast day of Saint George, the special holiday of the crossbowmen's guild (**Pl. 38**, p.44).

Closely related to the military companies were the chambers of rhetoric or literary guilds. Most of these were named after plants – *De Violieren* (gillyflower, pink), *Goudbloem* (marigold), *Olyftak* (olive branch). Their origins are obscure, but it is generally believed that they represented either a development from the staging of late medieval ecclesiastical plays or an offshoot of the military guilds' pageants. Their principal function was to organize literary contests (*landjewels*) between rival chambers of rhetoric. At these events a 'prince' would be elected who spoke the parting verse and set the rules for the composition and performance of literary set pieces which were often highly satirical in content.

In Venice the confraternities were similarly divided into a number of different categories with their membership embracing a wide range of Venetian society. The city had six major confraternities – the *Scuole Grandi* – the majority of whom began as flagellant brotherhoods, initiated in Italy by the great flagellant movement of 1260 (see Block I, Section 7). The origin of the Scuola di San Giovanni Evangelista, for example, is clearly indicated by the carved relief in the courtyard of the confraternity's meeting house (**Pl. 39**, p.45). Here the guardian of the Scuola and twelve of its members are shown in the habits of flagellants before their patron saint, Saint John the Evangelist.

While the *Scuole Grandi* might well have patricians amongst their members, Venetian noblemen did not hold office in these confraternities. This was the privilege of those Venetian citizens whose families, despite financial affluence and a long history of residence in the city, were nevertheless disenfranchised. As such the organization of the *Scuole Grandi* provides an example of one of the ways in which the corporate institutions co-operated with the governing élite of the city.

Apart from the *Scuole Grandi* there were a large number of *Scuole Piccole*. These might be formed by foreign communities in Venice such as the confraternity of the Dalmatians (Scuola di San Giorgio degli Schiavoni) and the confraternity of the Albanians (Scuola degli Albanesi). Alternatively, these minor confraternities might be dedicated to a particular cult like the innumerable *scuole del sacramento* attached to individual churches in Venice. Finally, there were the *scuole delle arte* organized by the various craft and trade guilds whose members were enrolled from these professional bodies.

As part of their social and institutional activities both the guilds and confraternities became important agencies for artistic patronage in each city. In order to perform their functions as commercial, administrative and welfare institutions, they required buildings. They also needed chapels or, at the very least, altars furnished with the requisite liturgical equipment in order to provide their members with a proper environment in which to perform their corporate acts of worship. The sort of art that these institutions commissioned was by necessity conditioned by such factors as the wealth of each institution, its priorities in the expenditure of its income, and the artistic practice of each city. In the following analysis of the artistic patronage of the principal corporate institutions of Antwerp and Venice, considerations of this sort will, therefore, be given some prominence.

The most impressive record of patronage, in terms of material resources and preservation of buildings and works of art, remains with the *Scuole Grandi* of Venice. In order to exemplify the kind of patronage practised by these institutions, the Scuola di San Giovanni Evangelista has been adopted as a model.

5.1 SCUOLA DI SAN GIOVANNI EVANGELISTA

Like a number of Venice's *Scuole Grandi*, the Scuola di San Giovanni Evangelista had a long history. Founded in 1261, it initially met at the church of Sant'Aponal, only transferring to the homonymous church of its patron saint, San Giovanni Evangelista, in 1307. A painting originally from the Scuola acts as a record of the façade of this tenth-century church (**Pl. 40**, p.46). In 1340 a member of the Badoer family bequeathed to the confraternity the upper floor of a hospital (originally founded by his family) adjacent to San Giovanni Evangelista. The inscription on the relief (**Pl. 39**, p.45) records that between 1349 and 1354 the confraternity reconstructed these premises in order to accommodate their charitable and devotional activities.

In 1369 Philippe de Mézières, Grand Chancellor of the kingdom of Cyprus, presented the guardian of the Scuola with a highly prized relic – a fragment of the Cross (**Pl. 40**, p.46). The significance of this act should not be underestimated since in Venice the cult of relics was assiduously pursued. The city's prestige at home and abroad greatly benefited from its reputation as a depository of literally thousands of these relics: pieces of material matter which by virtue of their physical relationship with holy persons were deemed to have special spiritual qualities. Relics formed the focus of the city's great civic processions, and all the city's major institutions were zealous guardians of their own prized relics. The Scuola di San Giovanni Evangelista was deemed particularly fortunate since their relic of the Cross was apparently capable of a number of miraculous acts. Some of these were recorded in a series of late fifteenth-century paintings designed to decorate the walls of the oratory where the relic was kept within the Scuola building (see below). The Scuola also adopted the Cross as a symbol of its corporate identity.

By the early fifteenth century the Scuola, as a result of increased membership bringing with it new funds from entrance fees and pious donations, was able to enlarge its property. In 1414 it took possession of the whole of the hospital (while replacing it by a new hospital built on an adjacent site). Initially the task of renovation was confined to adapting the thirteenth-century hospital to the functional needs of the Scuola. In 1420, however, the brothers took the decision to embellish their newly extended headquarters with two cycles of paintings. Neither has survived, but one depicting scenes from the Old and New Testament was for the meeting hall (*Sala del capitolo*) and the other, with no specified subject, for the Oratory of the Cross. The latter room was also supplied with an altar and painted altarpiece.

The painter employed on these projects was Jacopo Bellini (active *c*.1424, d.1470/1), the head of *the* family workshop of painters in fifteenth-century Venice. In this context, it is of interest that in 1437 the confraternity had agreed to admit to its brotherhood free of charge those artists who had contributed to the construction and embellishment of their building. Jacopo and his sons Gentile (*c*.1429–1507) and Giovanni (*c*.1430/40–1516) were all members of this confraternity. In 1453 Jacopo also obtained from the Scuola twenty ducats for the dowry of his daughter Nicolosia, who married another well-known painter, Andrea Mantegna (active 1451/5, d.1506).

In 1454 the Scuola enriched its lateral façade by a series of windows whose pointed arches and ornament are typical of much of fifteenth-century Venetian architecture. In the last decades of the century, however, the Scuola employed two architects to introduce a number of more innovatory features to their building. Between 1478 and 1481 Pietro Lombardo (*c*.1435–1515) executed a marble entrance portal for the Scuola's courtyard (**Pl. 41**, p.46); this portal has also been depicted to the left of the church in **Pl. 40** (p.46). On 14 August 1498 the brothers jointly agreed to the construction of a new internal staircase (**Pls 42, 43**, p.47). The architect of some of Venice's finest late fifteenth-century buildings, Mauro Codussi (*c*.1440–1504), received the commission for this project and was admitted to the Scuola free of charge. The staircase was designed to encompass the entire length of the Scuola building, and Codussi took advantage of the irregularity of the pre-existing walls to make it wider at the top (380 cms) than at the bottom (310 cms). The effect achieved is one of greater amplitude and grandeur (**Pl. 42**).

By these architectural additions the Scuola gained, first, an entrance portal which provided a clear indication of its identity and the extent of its property (**Pl. 41**). In the case of the second, it acquired a magnificent entrée to the building's principal rooms and an apt scenographic setting for the processions which featured prominently in the corporate life of the Scuola (**Pls 42, 43**). In terms of its costly materials (marble with porphyry and serpentine inlay) and its well-articulated vocabulary of classicizing detail, the staircase is representative of Venice's principal public buildings and the best of its Renaissance architecture.

In the sixteenth century, refurbishment of the exterior of the building continued with the redesigning of the ground floor windows and the provision of a new entrance doorway. As in the case of Codussi, this work was assigned to architects who had already proved their abilities on state projects such as the ducal palace. As for the interior, the Oratory of the Cross was refurbished at the turn of the century by a new cycle of paintings (see below). In the early sixteenth century, the Albergo (the room where the executive council met) was furnished with carved wooden stalls, and in the years immediately prior to 1544 Titian (*c*.1487–1576), by then Venice's leading painter, completed (with the assistance of his workshop) a series of paintings for the ceiling of this room with the *Vision of Saint John the Evangelist on Patmos* as its centrepiece (**Pl. 44**, p.48). In the last decades of the sixteenth century, Jacopo Bellini's cycle of paintings in the principal meeting hall was replaced by another series depicting scenes from the life of Saint John. The late sixteenth century was a time of great prosperity for the Scuola with Philip II of Spain, Don John of Austria, and the ambassadors of Spain and England becoming members of this confraternity.

Out of the eight paintings executed between *c*.1494 and 1510 for the Oratory of the Cross, three carry the signature of Gentile Bellini. It is generally assumed that Gentile was in overall charge of this project, supervising the designs of four or five other painters. The paintings depict variously the presentation of the relic to the brothers (**Pl. 40**, p.46) and a number of miracles which were reputed to have happened in Venice while the relic was in the Scuola's possession. Five paintings represent incidents where individuals were apparently healed by some form of contact with the relic in its ornate gold reliquary. Another depicts an incident when the reliquary fell into a canal and would only be received into the hands of the guardian of the Scuola, Andrea Vendramin (**Pl. 45**, p.49). In recognition of its acquisition from Cyprus, Caterina Cornaro, the Queen of Cyprus (exiled by the Venetian state to the small Italian hill town of Asolo in 1489), is portrayed with her retinue on the left bank of the canal.

As we have seen, in at least one of the paintings from the cycle, certain devotional and political concerns of the Scuola and Venice itself have been registered. Now examine the illustration of another painting from the cycle (**Pl. 46**, p.50). What exactly do you think this painting represents?

DISCUSSION

The painting first and foremost appears to depict one of the great ceremonial processions which featured so prominently in Venetian civic life. Its location is in the Piazza San Marco with the basilica acting as a magnificent backdrop to the scene. The white robed members of the Scuola carrying their reliquary of the Cross have been given a pre-eminent position in the long procession. Behind them and to the right of the composition appear the Venetian political hierarchy – doge, senators, ambassadors and other officials together with friars and priests. On the left, patrician ladies in low-cut dresses appear as spectators at the window of the building. Elsewhere in the square are other representatives of Venice's cosmopolitan society – children, a dwarf, a Moor, turbaned Turks and Greeks in their black brimmed hats.

Somewhat surprisingly, the supernatural event involving the relic of the Cross is entirely enveloped by this highly detailed depiction of civic and ceremonial display. Just behind the brothers carrying the reliquary under its canopy appears an elderly figure on his knees (**Pl. 46**). He represents a Brescian merchant, Jacopo de' Salis, who on 25 April 1414, the feast day of Venice's patron saint, Saint Mark, made a petition to the relic on behalf of his gravely sick son. As a result of his appeal, it was believed that his son was cured.

EXERCISE

Please look now at **Col. Pl. 6** (p.119) and repeat the same exercise as above.

DISCUSSION

Compared to Bellini's painted narrative, Carpaccio's painting represents a clearer illustration of an incident involving the brothers of the Scuola and their miracle-working relic. Even without precise information about the nature of this miracle, it is possible to observe some kind of dramatic encounter taking place on the upper loggia of the canalside building on the left.

Nevertheless, this narrative event has to compete with a plethora of other intriguing detail. Those of you who are familiar with Venice may recognize the location of the scene as the Grand Canal with the famous Rialto Bridge (albeit in its original wooden form) in the right-hand background. Once again the ethnographic variety of Venice's society has been depicted together with an immensely informative record of the physical environment of the city and daily life – painted polychrome façades, decorative chimney pots, a man repairing roof tiles, laundry hanging out to dry and a woman beating a carpet on an open air terrace, to mention only a few.

Set within this web of highly naturalistic detail is, yet again, a portrayal of an incident of particular significance for the brothers of San Giovanni Evangelista. In 1494 the Patriarch of Grado (a high-ranking ecclesiastic in the Venetian religious hierarchy), with the assistance of the Scuola's relic, had claimed to exorcise a demon that had taken possession of a young man. It was this act of exorcism that Carpaccio's painting was designed to commemorate.

While the topographic detail of both these paintings is visually compelling, it is odd that the focus of the painted narrative appears so incidental. Bellini likewise places the reliquary at the centre of his composition, but the dramatic encounter between Jacopo de' Salis and the relic is engulfed by the surrounding figures and ambience. Carpaccio utilizes a certain range of expressive gesture and pose to draw attention to the primary narrative incident, but counters it by the lively detail taking place on the canal itself. The use of tiny areas of vibrant colour set against the dark green of the canal further contributes to this effect.

Have these painters not really succeeded, therefore, in gratifying their patrons' desire for a series of paintings representing significant events in the devotional life of the Scuola? From the contents of Venetian chronicles, it is clear that Venetians kept detailed records of their political and religious triumphs. It appears, moreover, that paintings were envisaged as a kind of historic record of the veracity of these events. By supplying two paintings that were comprehensive in their descriptive detail, Bellini and Carpaccio had provided the Scuola with just the kind of 'truthful record' they needed in order to impress upon the brothers, and the world at large, the miracle-working properties of their prized relic.

In short, the Scuola di San Giovanni Evangelista as a confraternity of great antiquity and prestige (due in no small part to its ownership of the relic of the Cross) was able to attract large numbers of members, many of whom belonged to Venice's wealthiest and most illustrious families. By the late sixteenth century foreign princes also figured in its brotherhood. Through its membership, the Scuola was also able to command large material resources. It gradually increased the scale of its property and continuously took steps to enlarge and modernize its building, employing at the same time artists of the highest calibre. In terms of the building's architectural features and interior decor, the Scuola thus sought to present itself to the outside world as an institution worthy of great respect.

5.2 SCUOLE DELLE ARTE

By comparison, the artistic projects funded by the Venetian *scuole delle arte* were more modest. The location for their patronage tended to be a side altar in one of Venice's large number of churches. Here a particular *scuola delle arte* would concentrate its limited resources on purchasing endowment rights over an altar, thereby ensuring that masses would be performed for the spiritual benefits of its members, living and deceased, and supplying the altar with liturgical furnishings. One priority would, therefore, be the acquisition of a painted or sculpted altarpiece.

From a recently compiled table of 56 altarpieces (either extant or documented) commissioned by these trade confraternities between *c*.1360 and 1610, it appears that the artistic patronage of this type of confraternity was not as negligible as had once been thought. Like the paintings acquired by the Scuola di San Giovanni Evangelista, these altarpieces tended to represent a blend of devotional and secular concerns. Thus, the Scuola di Beccai (butchers) had their altar at San Matteo, and in honour of the church's titular saint chose as the subject of their painted altarpiece the calling of Saint Matthew away from his profession as a money-lender to be a disciple of Christ (**Pl. 47**, p.51). In the case of the Scuola dei Sartori (tailors), who by the sixteenth century had acquired a meeting house at Santa Maria dei Crociferi, their altarpiece, while depicting the cult figures of the Madonna and Christ Child with saints,

displays the guild's trade symbol of a pair of scissors prominently in the foreground (**Pl. 48**, p.51). It is also significant that the two painters commissioned by these trade confraternities, while competent, never worked on prestigious state projects like the ducal palace or one of the *Scuole Grandi*. They therefore commanded lower prices for their work.

From the evidence supplied by this group of altarpieces, other general observations can be made about the nature of the artistic patronage of the *scuole delle arte*. There was, on the whole, a tendency to employ somewhat old-fashioned formats such as polyptychs, which had been abandoned in the most advanced examples of sixteenth-century Venetian altarpieces. There was also a reliance on stock formulas, which would further suggest a conservative taste on the part of the clients.

5.3 GUILDS IN ANTWERP

Whereas in Venice the surviving evidence suggests a committed form of artistic patronage from both the major and minor confraternities – however much it might vary in scope and degree – in Antwerp it appears that the guilds took the greater initiative. However, since these two types of corporate institution were so closely integrated in terms of membership and social activities, it would be unwise to be too dogmatic on this point.

Guicciardini in his *Description of Antwerp* (1567) remarks on the impressive number of buildings in the city, both public and private. Amongst the specific examples he cites is the trade hall of the butchers' guild. This building, known as the Vleeshuis, is situated on the edge of the Burcht, which constitutes the oldest part of the city (**Pl. 49**, p.52). In point of fact, part of the building stands on an arch built over what was once the moat of the Burcht (**Pl. 50**, p.52). Unlike the Scuola di San Giovanni Evangelista who had to adapt a thirteenth-century hospital building to meet their ever-growing requirements, the butchers' guild was able to build from scratch, a remarkable feat in a city where land was scarce. As in the case of the Scuola, this wealthy and well-established trade guild employed the leading architect of the city, Herman de Waghemakere, to design and execute the building. As a measure of his expertise, this architect, together with his son Dominic, was responsible for the completion of the city's cathedral by the construction of the dome of the crossing and the upper part of the north tower.

The Vleeshuis presents a very different style of architecture from that of its Venetian counterpart. Built in brick, the exterior is embellished by regular courses of red brick and white stone. The high stepped roof is enclosed by a handsome gable. The side walls are marked out by buttresses surmounted by hexagonal turrets with spires. The building's large windows display a complex tracery of stone (**Pls 49, 50**). On the ground floor is a great hall vaulted in brick and subdivided by a row of sturdy piers (**Pl. 51**, p.53). Until the 1840s this hall continued to function as a market hall for the sale of meat. On the first floor another vaulted room, panelled in wood, once acted as a council chamber for the executive body of the guild.

What is lacking today, in its present guise as a museum, are the original furnishings which were once undoubtedly very lavish. In 1520, for example, the guild of Saint Luke entertained Dürer in their guild hall, known like so many of Antwerp's buildings by a particular name, the 'fur cloak', and situated in the city's principal square. On the testimony of the honoured guest, 'all their service was of silver and they had other splendid ornaments and very costly meats'. Thus, while the Vleeshuis might lack the classicizing form of certain of the architectural features of the Scuola di San Giovanni Evangelista, it too constitutes an impressive building in terms of its technical construction, uniformity of style and one-time interior embellishment.

A number of other houses of the trade and military guilds and chambers of rhetoric are located in the vicinity of the town hall, or Stadhuis, in the Grote Markt. On the ground floor were, and in number of cases still are, shops. On the south-west corner of the square, the series of narrow but very tall gable fronts, situated cheek by jowl, present a characteristic example of the form that these trade buildings once took (**Pl. 52**, p.54). One of these buildings, begun in 1579 for the coopers' guild and extended in 1623, displays the kind of classicizing ornament adopted by the city's builders in the latter half of the sixteenth century. The use of pediments and a type of decoration consisting of interlaced forms similar to cut leather and known as a strapwork was a style of architecture much favoured in the Netherlands at that time (**Pl. 53**, p.54). The original function of the coopers' house is clearly advertised by the series of reliefs depicting the tools used in the barrel-making trade (**Pl. 54**, p.55). On the gable of the adjacent building the roundels decorated with

crossbows similarly identify the building as the one-time hall of the military guild of the *arbalestriers* (**Pl. 55**, p.55).

As in the case of Venice, a major type of corporate patronage was the endowment of altars and commissioning of altarpieces to embellish them. Many of these painted and sculpted altarpieces were broken up by specific requests of the guilds in the second outbreak of iconoclasm that hit the city between May and June 1581. There is, however, one example of a guild altarpiece commissioned in 1508 which escaped the iconoclasts, providing visual evidence of the form that these guild altarpieces might take.

Like the Portinari altarpiece (see Block I, Section 8), this guild altarpiece is a triptych (**Pl. 56**, p.56) with the Lamentation over the dead Christ as its central image (**Col. Pl. 7**, p.120) and two narrative scenes from the legends of Saints John the Baptist and Evangelist on the interior surface of the wings (**Pls 57, 58**, p.57). These two saints reappear on the outer surface of the wings in the guise of fictive statues (**Pl. 59**, p.58).

The altarpiece was commissioned in 1508 from the painter Quinten Massys by the guild of the altarpiece-joiners or shrineworkers. Massys (1466–1530) came from Louvain but had registered in 1491 as Master in the Antwerp guild of Saint Luke. Like Bellini in Venice, he was a well-established painter. As a measure of his social status, he owned two houses in the city which were considered landmarks in his lifetime. One was called the 'The Ape' and was visited by Dürer on his 1520 visit. The second, known as 'Saint Quinten', had a polychromed statue over the doorway, and its façade, according to one seventeenth-century source, was splendidly decorated by Italianate ornament.

As in the case of the *scuole delle arte* in Venice, the shrineworkers were apparently anxious to acquire a traditional format for their new altarpiece. Originally the guild had been joined with the coopers' guild, and from 1456 the two guilds shared an altar in the cathedral of Antwerp. Their joint altarpiece had a similar subject as Massys' later altarpiece for the shrineworkers. In 1497 the two guilds separated and the shrineworkers acquired their own altar in the cathedral. The guild first placed an order for a carved retable with two sculptors from Louvain; in 1503 they transferred the commission to two Antwerp sculptors; finally in 1508 they gave the commission to Massys, meanwhile instructing him to reproduce the subject of their earlier jointly-owned altarpiece.

Indeed, a certain conservatism is apparent in the pictorial treatment of the central painting as compared with the wings, which present a variety of exotic detail and physiognomic types (**Pl. 56**). In depicting this particular aspect of Christ's Passion, Massys had a powerful model in Roger van der Weyden's celebrated *Deposition from the Cross*, which was executed for the Louvain crossbowmen's guild (**Pl. 60**, p.59). Although Massys' painting is not a literal copy, the gold background of the earlier painting being replaced by a landscape setting, in terms of the figurative composition it is clearly an adaption of it (cf. **Pl. 60** and **Col. Pl. 7**, p.120). In one way, therefore, Massys was able to provide his clients with a strikingly familiar image but one that also offered something new.

The subject itself and Massys' particular treatment of it are highly appropriate given the kinds of religious devotions that once took place before this altarpiece. In the first place, the depiction of the dead Christ acts as a kind of visual analogy to the symbolic re-enactment of Christ's Passion in the celebration of Mass. Moreover, the precise placing of Christ's body within the pictorial scheme, extended across the entire width of the composition and with the face and upper torso turned in the direction of the worshippers before the altar, would have provided a strong stimulus to the kind of religious contemplation which became a central feature of the type of spiritual exercises practised by these confraternities. As a means of further encouragement, one of the guild's patron saints, Saint John the Evangelist, while traditionally present at the Crucifixion, has also been given a prominent position just above the outstretched arm of Christ (**Col. Pl. 7**).

The outside of the shrineworkers' guild altarpiece likewise presents a conventional format for north European altarpieces (**Pl. 59**). In subdued tones of brown and gold, the guild's two patron saints are represented with their traditional attributes: Saint John the Baptist with the lamb (a reference to his greeting to Christ: 'Behold the lamb of God', John 1:36) and Saint John the Evangelist with a chalice containing somewhat unusually a small dragon. This object alludes to the attempt on the saint's life by the Emperor Domitian, who ordered the saint to drink a cup of poisoned wine: when John took up the cup to obey, the poison departed in the form of a snake. Thus, when the altarpiece was closed as customary

on weekdays and non-feast days, the painted exterior would serve as a means of identifying clearly the shrineworkers' guild and their devotion towards their two patron saints.

The inner surface of these wings further celebrates the guild saints. On the left wing the painted narrative depicts Herod and his wife Herodias at the feast held on Herod's birthday. Before the couple appears Herodias' daughter, Salome, presenting the head of Saint John the Baptist on a charger (**Pl. 57**). On the instructions of her mother she had requested the saint's execution as a reward for dancing before Herod's guests (Mark 6:17–28).

On the right wing the painted narrative depicts the second attempt by the Emperor Domitian to take the life of Saint John the Evangelist by throwing the saint into a cauldron of burning oil (**Pl. 58**). The saint is reputed to have emerged unscathed from this ordeal. Both scenes thus allude to the death of Christ, which forms the central theme of the painted altarpiece. A number of other symbolic connotations are also implicit in the organization of this triptych (**Pl. 56**). John the Baptist, the last of the Old Testament prophets, is shown as a martyr to the faith but irrefutably dead. John the Evangelist as a representative of the new order is shown in a situation where he ultimately triumphs over death.

As in the case of the Venetian Scuola's painted cycle, these narrative paintings present a rich array of costume and physical type. Given Antwerp's prominence in international trade, particularly in the exchange of luxury goods, Massys probably did not need to go far to obtain models for details such as the brocades, ermine, jewels and metal artefacts portrayed in these paintings.

The overall impression given by the painted altarpiece of crowded figures, congested space, colourful costumes and exotic detail is typical of a number of Antwerp altarpieces produced in the first half of the sixteenth century. Many of these stylistic features also apply to the carved wooden retables which were part of a thriving export trade between Antwerp and the rest of Europe (**Pl. 61**, p.60). In these retables, large numbers of small detatchable figures carved in the round are grouped together within shallow settings. Details of these intricate sculpted compositions are picked out by colourful polychromy and gilding. Since the shrineworkers produced casements, frames and ornamental housings for these retables, the guildsmen were obviously familiar with this genre. Indeed, the guild had first intended to procure such a retable for their altar. It is, therefore, very likely that Massys' densely packed narrative scenes provide further evidence of the painter responding to the dictates of a particular brief for this guild altarpiece.

In the last analysis, the guilds and confraternities of the two cities share more similarities than differences in their artistic patronage. In Antwerp and in Venice these corporate bodies relied on art in a functional sense (be it for business or religious purposes) and as a means of self-advertisement. The greater the wealth of the individual corporation, the greater the likelihood of commissions for the building and embellishment of grand meeting houses and private oratories, with the city's most prestigious artists employed on these projects. In general, however, every corporate body would endow an altar in one of the city's numerous churches and embellish it with some form of religious image. One striking contrast lies perhaps in the style of art that procured in the two cities. Nevertheless, this was not a fixed commodity; both cities as international trading communities were subject to the importation of 'foreign' artistic ideas be they through the agency of either practitioners or the objects. Thus, both Codussi and Massys were not natives of the town in which they established a flourishing practice. Massys in Antwerp had access to Dürer's prints, while Gentile Bellini and Carpaccio were aware of both Flemish and Florentine paintings; all three painters translated their sources into their own distinctive idiom. What ultimately unites the works of art produced at the behest of the guilds and confraternities of Antwerp and Venice is the evident willingness on the part of the artists concerned to co-operate with their group patrons and adapt their stylistic vocabulary in order to meet the specific requirements of these corporate institutions.

6 DOMESTIC LIFE: HOUSING AND LIVING CONDITIONS

ROSEMARY O'DAY

What was it like to live in either of these two major cities in the late fifteenth and sixteenth centuries? We have already sketched in the background against which the public and commercial life of both cities was played – but what of the domestic scene?

If you refer back to Block I, Section 5, you will recall that we spoke of the existence of various forms of household organization in Europe. Some households were of a simple, dual generation type – conjugal households containing parents and children; others were much more complex, involving perhaps several generations or, where brothers shared a household, several parallel conjugal families. Generally speaking, England, northern France and the Netherlands seem to have been remarkably homogeneous in their pattern of household organization, with a low proportion of complex households and a majority of conjugal households. Complex multi-generational households were much more common in southern and eastern parts of Europe, including southern France and Italy, although it is still true that there were pockets of habitation where simple, conjugal households were the norm. It is important to note that these are generalizations. As historians study in detail more communities, they often find exceptions to these general, regional patterns. Moreover, the form of household often varied according to social grouping: aristocratic or upper bourgeois households appear to have been larger and more complex than those of the middling poor. Depending upon the social status of the householder, the household might also include both domestic servants and workpeople.

Venice, as David Englander has explained, was structured by status and class. But the pressure on living space may well have blurred the divisions. Although it is true that the richest patrician families lined the Grand Canal with their houses, the possibilities for flamboyance in architecture were restricted by the site, and not every house on the Grand Canal could be well located near the business area of the Rialto or the government district of St Mark's. But for many more patrician families there was no space on the canal – they had to rent or buy houses throughout the city. This meant that the division of the city into occupational zones was never rigid. Patricians were unable to dominate single parishes or even single streets. Patrician families were to be found even in the poorer districts of Castello (near the Arsenal) and Santa Croce. Because leases could only be for five years at a time, it was difficult for a patrician family to be sure that it had a secure dynastic base in a given location. This may have removed the incentive to embellish or improve the accommodation. The pressure on space meant that even patrician dwellings were small and modest. In other respects, also, the physical conditions in Venice removed the opportunity for excessive display – there were no horses and carriages; everyone travelled on foot or by gondola or barchetta; there was little room to accommodate servants. This may well have fed the Venetian emphasis upon personal frugality noted by Peter Burke (1974). It is important to remember this. There is evidence of extremely luxurious living among the Venetian patriciate, but this was very much the exception and not the rule. It was also more marked when comparisons are made with the style of life of other urban patriciates.

If the patricians lived in relatively cramped conditions, the bourgeoisie, artisans and poor were even harder hit by the high rents and the insecurity of the property market in the city. Their only comfort must have been the generally high levels of employment in the city throughout the century. Food was generally in good supply and cheap; beggary was rare; the board of public health concerned itself with the city's hygiene in areas which affected everyone – rich and poor.

While access to Antwerp was allowed only through its six gates, one must not imagine the city as rising out of an area barren of inhabitation. Until the early 1540s houses were built right up to the walls both inside and outside the city. Many Antwerp citizens lived in rooms actually inside the city walls. In 1543 Charles V ordered that a zone of 1,400 yards be cleared of permanent buildings and trees on the outside of the walls (see Map 2). After this time Antwerp's separation from the surrounding countryside was more marked physically.

Population explosion was accommodated within the line of the medieval walls. The number of houses in the city mushroomed: 3,440 in 1437, 5,673 in 1480, 6,798 in 1496, 8,270 in 1526 and 13,500 in 1560. The area of Nieuwstad, incorporated in 1542, was developed as an industrial area and attracted little residential building.

So the sixteenth century saw the building and rebuilding of old Antwerp to accommodate the expanding population. The last gardens in the old nucleus of the city within its ring of moats and canals were parcelled out for building. In 1547 Van Schoonbeke, the speculative builder, developed a new quarter in the gardens of the Huis van Spangen by laying out the Friday Market (Vrijdagmarkt) and its surrounding streets. These were quickly lined with houses. Residents in the area continued to build new housing for rental. Christopher Plantin, who owned a house with a garden on the Friday Market, built four houses for rental on Holy Ghost Street. The cathedral administrators cleared away the art dealers who were in business between the churchyard and the Lombardenvest to build dwelling houses for rental. Houses were put up anywhere and everywhere within the old nucleus. New public buildings were forced into the newer sections of the city towards the walls. Citizens who wanted more space to live in also gravitated towards the walls. Residential expansion outside the old nucleus was also intensive and soon there were no large open spaces left; nevertheless, density here was lower and many houses boasted large gardens and courtyards.

Building of new accommodation could not keep pace with this growth, and there was great pressure on available housing and consequent high prices. Houses were tightly packed together. The middling ranks of society lived in two-storey houses, the rest in houses with one storey and an attic. Much of the accommodation in houses belonging to the prosperous was devoted to work purposes; private accommodation of a cramped variety was found for the head of the household and the members of his family, for business employees and their families, for maids and servants, for unmarried journeymen, and for paying lodgers. The type of extended household run by Christopher Plantin was not unusual in Antwerp: he accommodated the burgeoning families of his daughters and sons-in-law in far from commodious apartments. Poorer people rented rooms even in the old walls and guardhouses.

The available land dictated the architecture of new housing. Plots were narrow and houses were similarly narrow and had little depth. They possessed the steep stairs characteristic of Netherlandish housing. Because dwellings were now packed more tightly together, the wooden construction and thatched roofing popular in the fifteenth century was frowned upon. Preventative measures were taken by the civic authorities: from 1503 the thatching of roofs was forbidden; after 1546 a prohibition was placed upon building wooden house gables or repairing or replacing old ones. The shelter boards which hung out above windows and doors were restricted in overhang and had to be slated or covered in other non-flammable materials. Citizens were ordered to place barrels of water outside their street doors to help combat fire, a very real hazard in such cramped conditions.

The face of residential Antwerp certainly changed during the century. The city was crowded. Wooden buildings were fast giving way to brick-built structures (although there were still many wooden houses). Prosperous merchants built watchtowers on their houses or in their gardens as a status symbol. Some medieval features still remained, however – windows were only partly glazed; shutters were drawn across the lower parts in bad weather. And the domestic interiors of the houses seem to have been somewhat austere. Heating was primitive. Open hearths burning peat and wood were commonplace and not very effective. Some of the rich reserved well-insulated rooms as 'stoven' for cold days. In the winter when life on the street was difficult, it must have been singularly cold and cheerless within Antwerp's houses.

We have, however, to try to dismiss from our minds the idea that 'houses' were simply 'homes' in the modern sense. Many houses in sixteenth-century Antwerp were first and foremost workshops or sales outlets. An example which you have already met was the house of Christopher Plantin: most of the space in his house was devoted to the business; living accommodation was not high on his list of priorities. This was by no means unusual. Many houses had 'front boards' to display their wares. Houses were not numbered; instead they bore painted signboards giving the occupation of the inhabitant. When the occupants were not at work they were more often engaged in 'public' activities than domestic. Antwerp may not have presented as many grandiose opportunities for public display as Venice, but still her churches, her fairs, her processions, her guilds, her exchange, her brothels, her bath houses and her many drinking houses provided the focal points for citizens who were not 'at work'.

7 POSSESSIONS AND OWNERSHIP

CATHERINE KING

The public spaces of the cities of Antwerp and Venice belonged largely to the men who ran the government and presided over legislation and to the Church. As you saw in Section 5, these public spaces also belonged to the guilds and confraternities of the two cities, who built guild chambers and chapels and who congregated to express their aggregate strength and piety as workers. Women, by contrast, belonged in the home, taking no (or a very minor) part in the life of the guilds and confraternities. Paradoxically, the domestic interior and its wordly goods did not usually belong to them.

Spinsters could own goods and houses. Widows owned their dowry, and in addition would normally be granted the income of one-third to one-half of their spouse's property for their lifetimes. It was expected that the dowry would be willed to the widow's children. (In fact, some jurists held that the dowry was really the children's property of which the widow enjoyed the use.) Widows and spinsters comprised a very small section of the population. The majority of women were married, and all their goods were controlled by their husbands, except the contents of their wedding chest(s) and any clothes, books, jewellery or money which they had been given as personal gifts by their husband. A woman's relationship to the house she inhabited and the objects she used or which surrounded her as decoration was consequently more complex than a man's, depending upon her marital status and subject to alteration during her life-span. This situation offers an interesting contrast to the simple relationship of a man towards worldly goods, since after his majority he could own anything movable or immovable, acquiring and alienating it as he wished.

Within this pattern, the position of women in relation to worldly goods in Antwerp and Venice varied only a little. All over Europe, women who remained spinsters were allowed to stay outside the convent only if they were of the lower classes. Therefore, where the institution of monastic life remained secure, as in Venice, throughout this period young spinster noblewomen entered conventual life in which theoretically all goods were held in common. (In practice, as will be apparent from Block III, Section 12, some nuns in Benedictine houses could surround themselves with relative luxury.) In Antwerp women could control worldly goods more than they could in Venice. First, a widow had the right to take the choice items from the complete household goods, including what we would consider farm animals and implements, except for her husband's clothes. In Venice, even if a man willed his household goods to his wife, she was limited to taking only what she absolutely needed for food and drink. Second, women in Antwerp could inherit property over and above their dowry from the paternal family, while in Venice the dowry was held to cancel and prevent all patrimonial obligation to give property or other goods to daughters. In Flanders there were vestiges of the better legal treatment of women by Teutonic laws, while in Italy the poor position of women in Roman law had been made worse by a series of medieval communal laws designed to strengthen the patrimony and ensure its integrity.

The summary of the laws of the city of Antwerp issued by Plantin in 1582 (*Die Rechten ende Costumen van Antwerpen*) provides a list of the household goods that were legally due to either partner in a marriage at the death of the spouse (see *Anthology* II.3). This list assumes a relatively wealthy household in which the man belongs to a guild.

EXERCISE

Please pause and read this inventory, thinking about how the objects are gendered and about the picture we get of the domestic arrangements of someone quite well off.

DISCUSSION

This inventory is rich with information. There are, for instance, no forks mentioned, except for toasting, so we should infer that people ate with hands, knives and spoons. It is interesting that the woman, not the man, is associated with a book, that the nightclothes are considered 'unisex' (being mentioned in the first section of the inventory), and so are the *bandeaux* to keep the hair tidy. No such evidence exists in the printed Venetian laws, where the tone is acerbic:

> We declare that if any man shall leave his wife to be *madonna* in his house (that is to say by these words that she shall have the goods of the dead man) those things only shall she have, which are necessities relating to food and drink, according to the scope of the goods of the dead man...
>
> (*Index omnium in Venetiarum statutis continentur*, Venice, 1548, bk IV, ch. XV, pp.88–9, trans. C.E. King)

Venetian men did leave wives sizeable households, but clearly the statutes prevented the woman from choosing the best bed and the most attractive painting, let alone a silver drinking cup or a silver spoon, for herself to own as of right.

While women in prosperous households could be surrounded by luxurious goods, unless they were widows or spinsters they could not sell or buy them independently of their husbands. Wives of petty merchants could be in business in their own right, being treated as spinsters for contractual purposes, but this status applied strictly to their merchandise, not to their household. Women were, by and large, vicarious consumers, buying and selling as the unwaged stewards of their husbands.

Men composed the guilds of masons and woodworkers, who shaped domestic spaces both in Antwerp and Venice, and they were skilled in all branches of manufacture. They were therefore in a position to cast a critical eye over any of the products used in a household, and the building in which it was contained. Women, in comparison, laboured waged and unwaged at a narrower range of occupations, and consequently with a restricted power of discrimination concerning various products. Women made textiles – and clothing from them – out of linen, wool and silk. They were furriers and embroideresses handling gold thread, beads and feathers. They also made wigs and manufactured leather objects like belts, gloves, purses and bookbindings. Women were skilled in metalwork, making cutlery, pins, scissors, needles, and occupied in the trades of the goldsmith. They took part in the service industries of clothes washing, of food and drink preparation, and selling. A woman could therefore cast a practised eye over just such a range of goods and services.

It seems likely that women had a particular regard for the domestic interior because it was their job to cook household food and service the house; because their waged work often entailed labour in their homes; and because their lives were more restricted to the house, since the public spheres of group games and of government, in secular and ecclesastical life, did not belong to them. It will, of course, be evident that attitudes to worldly goods varied greatly depending on one's station in life, ranging from those who owned nothing but what they stood up in to those with large properties well stocked with the products of the skill of others. However, I think it is also important to stress that gender and marital status, just as much if not more than one's social class, affected one's ability to own or judge both worldly goods and the domestic interior.

Building ground in Venice was at an even greater premium than in Antwerp, because Venice was constructed on a series of mud islands. In Venice domestic buildings were even more crowded and every metre of space was utilized, with rooms often built out over narrow alleyways. In Antwerp many houses had adjacent gardens. In Venice (four kilometres from the mainland) ground was too precious for such a luxury. Any inner courtyard had to be paved so as to provide the run-off which gave Venetians their water supply. But in both cities housing shared the characteristics of being noisy (wooden partitions subdivided living space and there were no carpets), of lacking privacy for individuals (rooms led one into another), and of lacking different spaces for different tasks. Both cities had a rich manufacturing base, producing fine ceramics, glass, metalwork, wooden furnishing, textiles and leatherwork, although there were slight differences in the kinds of goods locally made which were available for the domestic interior: for instance, lace-making was invented by women in Venice at this period. To match the undifferentiated spaces of the house, furnishings were multi-purpose – the stool, for example, being designed so that it also acted as storage or could form a small table or desk. Furnishings were solidly built; items like clothes would be willed on to the next generations. Benches were often built-in and also shelves and cupboards. Such items which nowadays would form movable goods were part of the buildings. Tables were made so that they would fold, and be pushed back to a wall when not in use. Secondary beds were similarly designed so that they could be stored beneath the main bedsteads during the day. Only the richest owned chairs, most people sitting instead on benches or stools. In illustrations from Antwerp and Venice, and despite the warmer climate of the latter, the fireplaces dominate the rooms as if signifying the value placed on their provision of food and warmth.

Antwerp and Venice were capable of sustaining a small number of rich male collectors of art objects. This phenomenon marks a crucially important watershed in consumer history connected with the development of capitalism. Collectors initiated the patterns of behaviour which led to artists painting for public and private galleries and selling through agents and exhibitions. These domestic collections supported a trend already established in Italy in connection with religious and political commissions. This trend created a new identity for painters: from being craftsmen organized in workshops, they came to be seen as individual artists solving aesthetic problems. And their output gradually changed from mere craft and trade to the

status of art. Such collectors are documented a little earlier in Venice than in Antwerp, though the fact that in Antwerp painters were producing panels specifically designed for domestic settings (small moralizations of everyday life and townscapes, small illustrations of scenes from the Bible, ancient history, mythology) suggests that the collecting habit in Antwerp was well established. Such collections opened up new markets, since the works did not require quite the lofty political or religious significance of large commissions in town hall, convent or church.

The earliest Antwerp collection to be inventoried is that of Michiel van der Heyden, recorded in 1552. In the preamble he is described as *Ritter* ('Knight'). Pause and read this inventory (*Anthology* II.4). Note how many subjects are secular.

Most scenes were biblical ones. In a few instances the inventory names the painters (the local artists Quinten Massys and Hieronymus Bosch). The collection is exclusively local except for the painting of 'the black chiefs', and it proves more concern with subjects than with personal styles.

It is interesting to compare this collection with that of Andrea Odoni, whom Lotto portrayed in 1527 surrounded by his treasures (**Pl. 72**, p.67). The artistic worldly goods of this Venetian banker are recorded not only in the inventory of his son's possessions (Andrea's wife had been merely their 'caretaker' during her lifetime on condition that she passed them to her son), but also in the description of them – and many other collections in the Veneto – made by Marcantonio Michiel in the 1530s (see *Anthology* II.6).

In contrast to that of Michiel van der Heyden, Andrea Odoni's collection contained a large variety of ancient Roman and Greek sculpture and medals, along with cups and vases carved by modern Italian artists from porphyry and crystal. It also contained porcelain and objects of curiosity from faraway places (petrified crabs, fishes, snakes, lizards, a chameleon and crocodiles). Most of the paintings were by Italians, and attribution to individual artists was more frequently given. There was the portrait of the collector (**Pl. 72**), and there was rather less emphasis on sacred subjects. There were one French painting and two Flemish ones. These differences are in part to be explained in terms of the interests developed during the fifteenth century in Italy both in the cult of artistic personality and in ancient art.

The notion of the superiority of Italian culture depended on two things. First was her possession of the greatest fund of artefacts of antiquity; second was the creation in the fifteenth century by Florentines of the new science of perspective. This cultural hegemony led Antwerp to follow all things Italian during the sixteenth century, which is evident in a comparison of interiors illustrated in the fifteenth and sixteenth centuries. The gothicizing modes of the earlier period have been superseded by the glamour of classicizing articulation.

It seems unlikely that many people in Antwerp had access to more than a few items of this Italianate style, since they were inhabiting domestic interiors which had to have 'built-in longevity'. Only the very rich had the resources to adopt Italian styles in a thoroughgoing way.

EXERCISE

Look at the six pairs of illustrations: **Pls 62–63, 64–65, 66–67, 68–69, 70–71, 72–73** (pp.61–7). Suggest ways in which you can compare the domestic scales and worldly goods of Antwerp and Venetian people in the sixteenth century. You should note that paintings are often of a religious or other subject, which the setting, props and costumes are primarily tailored to illustrate. They are categorically not reportage. Further, the genres of representation in Antwerp which show aspects of ordinary life – as, for example, *The Cook* (**Pl. 74**, p.68) – have no equivalent in Venice.

DISCUSSION

Pls 62 and **63** (p.61) show that elaborately painted house fronts were equally used to display wealth: in Venice of a Flemish merchant and in Antwerp of the grand house of Cornelis de Vriendt. Both cities had men of upper- and middle-class status who could show off cultured taste.

Pls 64 and **65** (pp.62–3) show interiors, one Flemish and one northern Italian, demonstrating the simplicity of furnishings as filtered through the representation of a religious scene. In the fifteenth and early sixteenth century interiors would be normally quite stark.

However, **Pls 66** and **67** (p.64) demonstrate the lavish interior decoration and worldly

possessions available to an abbot in Flanders and a young ecclesiastic in Venice. No illustrations of abbesses show personal luxury. These clerics possessed an opulence known otherwise only to wealthy merchants or city leaders.

Pl. 68 (p.65) provides a Venetian illustration of an interior arranged to demonstrate the home life of Mary. **Pl. 69** (p.65) shows the palatial interior planned by Hans Vredeman de Vries to make the setting for Christ in the House of Martha and Mary. It seems that during the sixteenth century expectations of owning more worldly goods increased, and the Italianate, classicizing style spread northward to Flanders.

Pls 70 and **71** (p.66) show the way Venetian and Antwerp painters were asked to celebrate marriage in images of concord and reciprocal giving, and clothed in choice garments and rich surroundings. The domestic interior for the lay person was the site of the family. Above all, the family meant the transmission of worldly goods to healthy male heirs. Artists celebrated this handing over and handing down of the patrimony in images which offer us diagrams of family order and evidence of the wealth thereby secured.

Pls 72 and **73** (p.67) show art collections in Venice and Antwerp, the representations being separated by a century. We noted that collectors are documented earlier in Venice than in Antwerp. So it is no surprise to find that the collectors themselves were portrayed earlier in Venice too.

Pl. 74 (p.68) shows Pieter Aertsen's *The Cook*, dated 1559 on the mantelshelf. It demonstrates the homely and strong items you will have noted in the Antwerp inventory, and also – in the classicizing architecture of the fireplace – the new Italianate styles which swept Flanders. There are no illustrations of this sort in Venetian painting of this period, and this absence may indicate a different relationship to worldly goods. But despite some significant differences between the communities, the general impression is of a similarity both in the meaning of worldly goods to women and men, and in their distribution across the classes of Antwerp and Venice.

PART THREE
HUMANISM

8 BESSARION AND PAUWELS

LUCILLE KEKEWICH

8.1 PRIVATE AND PUBLIC BOOK COLLECTING

Throughout the Middle Ages some monasteries had owned substantial numbers of books, but it was a comparatively recent development for individuals to have large libraries. In the fifteenth century major collections were acquired by Cosimo de' Medici, Pope Nicholas V and Duke Philip the Good of Burgundy. The increase in lay literacy and the introduction of printing encouraged more people to collect books during our period. The late fifteenth century in both Antwerp and Venice saw individual initiatives which linked book collecting with civic consciousness and prestige. A study of two bequests should illuminate the nature and purposes of contemporary book collecting, as well as some of the similarities and differences between scholarly activity in Antwerp and Venice.

Pensionary (a legal advisor to a city, rather like an English Recorder) Pauwels left his collection of books to the City of Antwerp. His executors, who had effected their transfer, were discharged by the letter which records his bequest on 5 April 1481. Antwerp together with most of the rest of the Low Countries had recently passed into the Habsburg sphere of influence through the marriage of its duchess, Mary of Burgundy, to the Emperor Maximilian. The replacement of the Valois dukes – notable patrons of art and literature – by a dynasty not, at that stage, renowned for its love of learning had little impact on the cultural life of the Flemish towns. Their robustly independent attitude to their rulers throughout the previous century was reflected in their town records, their processions (*Ommegangen*) and their festivals as well as in their periodic rebellions against authority. The modest list of 41 books left by Pauwels contains no evidence of being influenced by the French taste which had predominated at

the court. The provisions made for keeping the books were entirely concerned with local conditions and needs; they made no reference to external ducal or imperial authority.

EXERCISE

Read *Anthology* II.7 and answer the following questions:

1 What provisions were made for keeping the collection of Pauwels for the city?

2 What impression do you get concerning the interests of Pauwels from the list?

DISCUSSION

1 After the books had been carefully checked against the inventory, they were to be placed in a room (presumably in the town hall). The counsellors, secretaries and clerks of the city government could use them but they were not to be lent, hired out or sold.

2 All the original titles were in Latin, and no indication is given that books of any other language were present in the collection. A few books cannot be classified – 'a small volume', for example. Of the remainder, nearly half were law books: 19 out of a total of 41. They can be identified because they refer either to ancient collections of canon and Roman civil law – the *Decretals* and the *Digest* – or to well-known legal writers such as Bartolus and Tancredus. The remaining works fall into a number of distinct categories. The Bible, the *Catholicon* (a dictionary), and the *Etymologies* (an encyclopedia by St Isidore of Seville) were commonly to be found in medieval book collections. The same could be said of the *Vegetius* (a military manual) and the compendium of advice for kings and princes. Valerius Maximus' collection of anecdotes and stories about ancient Rome was also very popular with lay and clerical readers. Together with the *Story of Troy* it catered for a taste Pauwels seems to have had for history. Works by Seneca and Cicero could be found in many collections of traditional authorities, but in this case it is interesting that they were joined by the works of Italian humanists such as Lorenzo Valla, *Eneas, Of Two Lovers* (a text by Aeneas

Sylvius Piccolomini, later Pope Pius II) and Gasparini. The *Rhetoric* of Cicero was a conventional enough guide for a lawyer to possess, but the attached commentary by Gasparini had only been produced a few decades earlier. A further indication that Pauwels was receptive to new ideas is that nine of his books were described as being printed. Printing was only established on any significant scale in the Netherlands in the mid-1470s. Yet he was prepared, during the last years of his life, to add to his collection by almost 25 per cent by acquiring printed books. You may have noted that, apart from the Bible, no religious works are recorded in the list. Pauwels may well have retained service books for the use of his family, but he seems to have had no time for lives of the saints and the Virgin or for the *devotio moderna*. Taking his interest in humanist scholarship and printed books together with the project to leave his books to the city of Antwerp – a move for which no precedent is recorded – it would not be claiming too much for this obscure lawyer that he was a true innovator, influenced perhaps by Italian ideas of eloquence and nobility as well as by local Brabantine traditions of civic pride.

A great deal is known about the gift of Cardinal Bessarion's library to the city of Venice; this contrasts with the scanty information available concerning the bequest by Pauwels.

Figure 24   Tobias Stimmer, Portrait of Bessarion, *engraving, from P. Giovio,* Elogia Virorum Illustrium, *Basle, 1577. Reproduced by permission of the British Library Board.*

Read the extracts from the Papal Bull of 1467 and the Act of Donation of 1468 in *Anthology* II.8. Then list:

1   The justification Bessarion gave for book collecting.

2   The reasons for his decision to give his library to Venice.

3   The conditions under which the library was to be administered.

DISCUSSION

1   From boyhood Bessarion had sought to acquire books in all disciplines. No treasure seemed to him to be more valuable than volumes full of the wisdom of antiquity, good customs, laws and religion. Without such examples there was a danger that men would be ignorant of human and divine affairs. Since the defeat of the Greeks and capture of Byzantium (a name often given to the whole of the Eastern Empire – 'Constantinople' eventually superseded 'Byzantium' as the name of its capital), he had made it his object to acquire as many Greek books as possible for posterity lest some should disappear altogether.

2   He feared that when he died his collection would be dispersed, so he decided to deposit both Greek and Latin books in one safe place for the use of the community. He considered all the towns of Italy and decided that nowhere was safer than Venice with its stable regime and moderate political system. It had seemed to Greeks like him, with its cosmopolitan atmosphere, to be a second Byzantium. He was grateful for the welcome he had received. For all these reasons he gave his library into the care of the procurators of St Mark's.

3   The books were to be deposited in a secure library in the vicinity of St Mark's. The cardinal would keep back a number of books for his own use during his lifetime. The public must have good access to the library so they could study the books in that place. No volumes should be sold or otherwise alienated and none should leave Venice. Loans should be allowed only against the pledge of adequate security.

Bessarion's background and career explain his anxiety that his library should endure and be deposited in Venice. He was born at the turn of the century in Trebizond, a busy port at the east end of the Black Sea and a centre for scholars and clerics. His early years were consequently spent in an environment which was not dissimilar to that of Venice. In adulthood he moved to Constantinople where he entered the monastic order of St Basil, changing his name from Johannis to Bessarion, the patron saint of Trebizond. He rose rapidly in the Church and became Archbishop of Nicaea and a useful servant of the emperor, John Palaeologus. The pressure of the Ottoman Turks on the empire had led many to believe that only the union of the Latin and Greek churches would invoke the kind of Western support that was required to ensure its survival. Bessarion, the patriarch of Constantinople and the emperor agreed on this policy and attended a council with the pope at Ferrara in 1438. It subsequently moved to Florence and there, despite the inconvenient death of the patriarch, a union was agreed by which the Eastern Church recognized papal supremacy. On his return to Byzantium the emperor discovered that the majority of the clergy and laity were not prepared to accept subordination to Rome: the small amount of military aid forthcoming from the West made the arrangement seem like a bad bargain from a practical as well as doctrinal point of view. Bessarion and some of his colleagues, however, were intellectually convinced of the merits of union. He may also have been attracted by the cultivation and security of the life he had experienced in Italy. The pope expressed his gratitude for Bessarion's support by making him a cardinal in 1439; in the following year he left Greece for good and took up residence in Rome.

'In Constantinople Bessarion was the most Latin of the Greeks, in Rome he became the most Greek of the Latins,' noted Lorenzo Valla (quoted by Vast, 1878, p.154). Bessarion's palace on the Quirinal became a principal centre for humanist studies and was sometimes referred to as his Academy. Italians like Poggio Bracciolini, Flavio Biondo and Lorenzo Valla and Greeks such as Theodore Gaza and George of Trebizond gathered there and received patronage from the cardinal. He became increasingly adept at reading and writing in Latin as well as Greek.

Another less tranquil aspect of the humanists' activity was their tendency to engage in vituperative controversies. On the whole Bessarion kept himself aloof from the encounters of belligerent associates like Poggio and Valla, and he attempted to calm their animosities. He could, however, scarcely ignore the violent attack launched by George of Trebizond against Plato, whom he compared unfavourably with Aristotle. Bessarion's book,

Against the Calumniator of Plato, dealt moderately and systematically with the charges brought by George of Trebizond. He claimed that admiration for the work of Plato did not necessarily imply a condemnation of Aristotle, who had, after all, been a follower of Plato. Some of the latter's ideas were fallacious – that the soul had an independent existence prior to the body, for example – but on the whole they either anticipated or coincided with Christian philosophy. He concluded: 'Plato is not only instructed and endowed with a truly divine genius, but he is as near as a pagan can be to the truth of Catholic dogma' (*Against the Calumniator of Plato*, bk II, ch. 13).

The general opinion in scholarly circles, including that of Marsilio Ficino in Florence, was that Bessarion had won the debate game, set and match. A positive result of the controversy was that the works of Plato were promoted and disseminated, and Bessarion's summary of his merits was printed soon after it was completed.

One of the greatest resources available to Bessarion for his humanist scholarship was the large collection of books he amassed. You will remember the first paragraph of *Anthology* II.8(B) stated that his bibliophile interests had started in childhood. His sojourns in various monasteries in Greece, and later his wealth and influence as a cardinal to whose palace many Greek scholars resorted, put him in a unique position to find and purchase or copy many of the major works of classical antiquity. When discussing the Greek and Latin authorities which were the concern of humanists, it must be recognized that many Roman writers had themselves been reliant on the work of their Greek predecessors, so we are by no means considering different cultural traditions. Bessarion did not confine his collection to Greek books; he needed a good acquaintance with the learning of his contemporaries in Italy to be able to engage in their concerns.

Bessarion took a close and solicitous interest in his books, often acquiring a second copy of a work if it seemed to be more accurate or was made in a pleasing fashion. He was certainly a bibliophile – that is, a lover of books as pleasing objects – as well as a collector. He inscribed most of his collection in his own hand with a shelf mark and indication of the contents and an *ex libris* such as 'Cardinal Nicenus'. Presumably the original marks reflected the arrangement of Bessarion's library in Rome; he subsequently changed some of them. It seems likely that he did this as part of his project to hand over his library to Venice. The titles were loosely arranged according to subject: texts of the Bible and commentaries came first, followed by devotional works, the Church Fathers, theology and canon law. The remainder of the shelf marks were given to books of civil law, philosophy, science, rhetoric, history, Greek poetry and grammar. Renaissance library books were usually displayed on lecterns and shelves or kept in chests. No specific information is available about the appearance of Bessarion's collection, but some idea of what it might have looked like can be derived from contemporary paintings (see **Pl. 75**, p.68).

You have already gathered from his eulogy of the city in *Anthology* II.8 why Bessarion decided to leave his library to Venice. He was anxious that the collection, which included rare texts that would be difficult to replace since the Turkish capture of Byzantium, should be deposited in a strong, politically stable city; but there were also other factors which determined his choice. The Venetians historically identified less closely with the ancient Roman Empire than did most contemporary Italians. They believed that they had gained their liberties independently of any Roman intervention. This tradition in conjunction with their geographical position gave them a strong political, cultural and economic predisposition to look to the East and, in particular, to Byzantium. During the 1460s Bessarion was heavily engaged in diplomacy, attempting to gain support from the Christian rulers of Europe for a crusade to recover Byzantium from the Turks. The Venetians had been his most active collaborators in this doomed enterprise and had given him a tremendous welcome when he returned from an unsuccessful legation to Germany in 1461, inscribing his name in their Golden Book as an honorary member of the Great Council. Bessarion viewed Venice as a successful and just aristocratic republic of which Plato would surely have approved. Patricians such as his friend Paolo Morisini, the state's ambassador to the papal court, attributed quasi-mythological origins to the state which were noble and inspiring. The encouragement of such beliefs was a common characteristic of the growth of civic and national consciousness at this time.

Bessarion, the philosopher-prelate, left his library to a state which most closely reflected his ideal form of government and which would be at the centre of any future initiative for recapturing Byzantium. Fortuitously, this coincided with a time when the Venetians were becoming increasingly predisposed to humanist studies:

> … the aristocracy came to realise … that Greek humanism was not only intellectually rewarding but could be utilized to serve the highest interests of the state.
>
> (Geanokoplos, 1963, p.39)

Several inventories of Bessarion's library survive, including the original one attached to his donation in 1468. That listed all the books then in his possession, although he retained a number of them for his own use during the remainder of his lifetime. The rest were packed off in chests and deposited in the Sala Novissima in a recently completed wing of the doge's palace. The next inventory was made in 1474, two years after the cardinal's death, when the books he had retained and a number he had acquired since the act of donation were received in Venice – about 1,024 altogether. It is 50 pages long in the modern edition and cannot, therefore, be quoted in full. A selection of titles has been made so you can get a feel for the nature of the collection: it is hoped that the choice of a representative balance of subjects reflects this. As far as possible, authors and titles of works have been chosen which have already been mentioned in the course material.

--- **EXERCISE** ---

Read *Anthology* II.9 and then note down:

1   The impression you gain of Bessarion's priorities and interests.

2   How does his collection compare with that of Pensionary Pauwels?

--- **DISCUSSION** ---

1   The strongest impression you are likely to have gained is that of the preponderance of Greek works. This is not surprising in the light of what has been established about Bessarion's background. The list certainly bears out his claim that he was preserving a classical heritage for posterity. (For example, a tenth-century manuscript of Homer's *Iliad* known to scholars as 'Venetus A' is still the main source for a definitive text.) Part of the library was composed of the service books, Bibles and works of the Church Fathers and Doctors of the Church that any great prelate could be expected to possess; he also had books by Latins such as Augustine, Gregory and Thomas Aquinas and by Peter Lombard, 'the Master of the Sentences', and by Greeks, Gregory Nazianzenus and John Chrysostom

(golden tongue). Bessarion's taste was truly universal: his own major disciplines were theology and philosophy and these were generously represented, but he also possessed authorities which covered all the main subjects studied in medieval universities (see Block I, Section 11). A number of books related to the cardinal's own controversial encounters, particularly George of Trebizond's *Against Plato* and his rejoinder *Against the Calumniator of Plato*. His interest in contemporary affairs is further demonstrated by *Of the Power of the Church* by Jean Gerson, a French chancellor and a prominent participant in the Conciliar Movement earlier in the century (see Block I, Section 9), and *On the Manner of Electing the Doge of Venice*. Apart from his ownership of a wide selection of good Greek and Latin classical texts, his humanist tastes are further illustrated by Leonardo Aretino's *The Italian War* and the *Geography* of Strabo annotated by Bessarion's master Gemistos Pletho. The 1474 catalogue was not compiled by Bessarion, but the practice of commenting on the appearance of some of the books was certainly taken from the earlier one of 1468 for which he was responsible. 'A new and beautiful book', 'in parchment, the best', 'not bound', 'a most beautiful volume' and 'covered with cloth of gold' are comments which provide a direct testimony to his solicitude for his books. One aspect of the collection which apparently did not particularly interest him was whether his books were printed since, unlike Pauwels, this was not noted although he did own a few.

2 You may have been surprised by the number of books that were owned by both Pauwels and Bessarion. The situation is distorted, of course, by the selective choice made from the latter's collection. The fact remains that some of Pauwel's legal books and nearly all the identifiable remainder of his collection were to be found in the cardinal's library. In an age when only a limited number of authoritative books existed, it could be expected that a great prince of the Church would own most of them. Yet it surely reflects rather well on Pensionary Pauwels that his small Antwerp collection contained such an interesting variety of titles. Perhaps he also showed his intellectual independence, unlike Bessarion, by shunning any of the traditional theological and devotional authorities of the Christian Church.

The 'secure location' envisaged in the 1468 Act of Donation where Bessarion's library was to be housed took nearly 100 years to materialize.

The books could have been accommodated reasonably well in the Sala Novissima in the ducal palace, but in 1485, still in their chests, they were stacked behind a wooden screen to save space. The sensible regulations controlling the borrowing of books were ignored. Those who managed to overcome the considerable problems of access sometimes stole volumes which were later offered for sale in the streets of Venice. Others kept books for excessive periods: one Leonico Tomeo held on to one for nearly 40 years. During the following decades the involvement of Venice in expensive wars and the failure of the procurators to show an interest in the collection contributed to its decline. The situation improved considerably from 1515 onwards when two humanists, first Andrea Navagero and then the even more distinguished Pietro Bembo, took over responsibility for the library as 'custodians' from the dilatory procurators. They pursued renegade borrowers (the former even had papal authority to threaten excommunication for those who did not return their books) and this policy gradually proved effective. In 1531 the cases were finally moved from the pile behind the screen in the ducal palace and transferred to an upper floor of St Mark's. There the books were unpacked at last and arranged on beautiful, purpose-built shelves (*plutei*) and lecterns. A few years later the procurators finally fulfilled the commitment to provide a 'secure library', and commissioned Jacopo Sansovino to build a public library opposite the ducal palace on St Mark's Square (see TV 5). At some point between 1559, when the shell of the building was completed, and 1565, when it was announced that the library would be closed every Maundy Thursday to protect it from the carnival crowd, the collection was installed in Sansovino's building.

It would be misleading to suggest that either Pensionary Pauwels or Cardinal Bessarion intended to found a public library as the term is currently understood. From the provisions of both bequests it seems that the donors had particular categories of users in mind. Pauwels probably expected that his collection of predominantly legal books would be used by city officials. Bessarion's intention appears to have been to provide humanists like himself with access to a large and well-arranged collection of Greek and Latin works. Despite the fact that limited categories of citizens were likely to profit from the book collections, both donations made an inherent assumption that they were for the benefit and enhancement of the cities to which they were made. 'The city' is referred to several times in the Pauwels bequest, and Bessarion praised Venice above all other Italian cities: 'governed with uprightness and wisdom; which is the home of virtue, self-restraint, dignity, justice and faith' (*Anthology* II.8).

9 PRINTING IN VENICE AND ANTWERP

NOEL COLEY

As we have seen, Bessarion's library was a Renaissance collection which consisted mainly of rare and beautiful manuscript books written in Latin and Greek. The library contained few printed books, although in the last 30 years of the fifteenth century Venice became the leading centre for printing in Europe, producing twice as many books as its nearest rival, Paris. No fewer than 4,000 editions representing at least a million books came from the Venetian presses in this period. The existence of so many books affected the life of the city itself, for by the 1490s rank upon rank of bookstalls offered their wares to the Venetian citizen walking from the Rialto to Piazza San Marco. Venice was the first city to feel the full impact of the invention of printing.

Most of the books printed in Venice in the 1470s and 1480s were meant to appeal to an established circle of readers. The demand for classical texts was strong, and editions of Virgil, Horace, the elegaic poets, the satirists and prose writers like Livy and especially Cicero were regularly produced. These works were sought by the many public and private teachers in the city as well as noble families and others in high positions. There was also a thriving export trade in these printed texts. In prestige, commercial value and sheer volume, however, all other kinds of publications in Venice were eclipsed by law books, which were expensive and yielded good profits although the capital investment by both printer and bookseller was high. The proximity of the Universities of Bologna, Padua, Pavia and Ferrara ensured the demand for law books, and some printers made fortunes out of them. For theological and liturgical texts, on the other hand, Venice lagged behind other European centres of printing, though there is evidence to suggest that editions of such works formed part of the printers' output before 1500. The increased volume of printed books meant that students could peruse the texts for themselves instead of merely listening to the master reading them aloud.

While these were the chief products of the printers' craft in fifteenth-century Venice, there were also those who wished to foster the spread of learning among ordinary people: pamphlets and the chap-books containing specimens of tales and ballads, hawked by pedlars, were produced cheaply and would be either quickly thrown away or used until they were worn out. Printers aimed for quantity and popularity, but the production of large numbers of such books aroused strong criticism.

Fra Filippo di Strata, a Dominican friar, was a virulent critic of printers who, he said, were ignorant vagabonds and idlers, snoring away the hours in a drunken stupor. He would have liked to see them banned from the city, for he thought they were getting above themselves and were a threat to the whole fabric of society. In particular, he thought they threatened the quality of scholarship and the texts they sold were hopelessly inaccurate, prepared by ignorant oafs and printed without correction. They drove out valuable manuscripts from the market and tempted uneducated fools to give themselves the airs of learned doctors. Printed books were so cheap that even children could afford them, and crafty printers, seizing their opportunity, produced books of pagan myths or Roman love poetry to titillate the erotic fancies of the young. Even religion was in peril, for as vernacular translations and cheap printed versions of the Scriptures which corrupted the beauty and subtle meaning of the Latin were circulated throughout society, simple people would be led astray towards heresy and damnation. As a dedicated scholar and purist Fra Filippo expressed his criticisms in extreme terms, but he was not alone for there were many who felt that the proliferation of books vulgarized learning.

Thus fifteenth-century Venice was a city in which books had become readily available and were being read by a wide cross-section of the ordinary people. It was into this situation that Aldus Manutius (1450–1515), the scholar who was to become the leading printer of Venice, came in 1490. He at once set out to produce reliable works of the Greek classics, a language which is technically difficult for the printer. Aldus gathered Greek scholars and compositors around him and made Greek the language of his household. During the years 1495–8 he issued five volumes of Aristotle and the comedies of Aristophanes, later followed by other Greek classics. To promote Greek studies Aldus formed an academy of Hellenists in 1500. Its rules were written in

Greek; its members were obliged to speak Greek and their names were Hellenized. They included Erasmus. Thus, within a couple of decades Aldus had done much to transform the image of the printer, and the Aldine Press set a high standard for its scholarly publications which was to be an example to other printing houses in Venice and elsewhere.

As a result of its long-established trading activities, Venice had the most advanced system of commercial distribution. Books printed in Venice were sold all over Italy and in Germany, France, Spain, the Low Countries, England and wherever there was a demand for printed books. During the decade 1471–80 centres of printing increased rapidly throughout Europe, mostly in towns which, like Venice, were successful in commerce. On the whole the university towns did not attract printers, but Cologne, Basel, Paris, Valencia and Naples – all thriving centres of trade, banking and the law – were also centres of printing. The presses which had the largest output in the late fifteenth century were at Cologne, Rome, Deventer, Nuremberg, Gouda, Milan, Florence and Antwerp, where printing was established in 1481.

Before the mid-sixteenth century there was little differentiation between the functions of the type-founder, printer, publisher, editor and bookseller. The same firm usually combined most or all of these crafts and trades. Printing and publishing had hardly outgrown the restlessness of the early practitioners who, needing little capital or equipment, were able to set up their presses almost anywhere, but the number of printers was growing and the days of small itinerant printers were numbered. Printing, publishing and bookselling were becoming separated, each needing capital, stability and forward planning. In Antwerp printers were often contracted to produce works for publishers in other places. Sometimes a printer had connections abroad. Heinrich Quentell, an Antwerp printer, became famous for his Low German Bible published in Cologne in 1479. Its many woodcut illustrations were reused in later German Bibles, notably the Nuremberg Bible (1483). All the early English Bibles were printed abroad. Tyndale's New Testament appeared in Cologne, Worms and Mainz, while his Hexateuch (the first six books of the Old Testament) was printed in Antwerp. Miles Coverdale's first complete English Bible came out in Antwerp in 1536. Many other books printed in English in the first half of the sixteenth century were produced in Antwerp, although works in English were also printed in

many other towns. In England there were very limited facilities for type-founding, and English printers were forced to purchase their type from abroad. One of the main sources for Roman and Italic type was Antwerp.

Thus, while Venice had been a centre for the book trade as a whole – printing, publishing and selling books – Antwerp concentrated mainly on the art and craft of printing. By 1550 the printing trades in both Germany and Italy had declined, and the lead was taken over by France and the Netherlands, where Antwerp was to become most important after the arrival of Christopher Plantin (see TV 4).

10 THE JEWS IN VENICE

DAVID GOODMAN

In the late fifteenth and sixteenth centuries tens of thousands of Jews fled from persecution in western and central Europe, settling mostly in Poland-Lithuania and the Balkans (see Block V, Section 6). A small part of this great exodus arrived in the city of Venice from Germany, Antwerp, Spanish Naples and above all from Portugal. Attracted there by the opportunities for trade and the freedom from persecution, the Jews found Venice to be a welcome refuge. But the lagoon was far from being a complete haven: Jews were much less harassed in the neighbouring duchy of Ferrara, in Poland and the Ottoman Empire.

Although Jews made up no more than $\frac{1}{2}$ to 1 per cent of the population of sixteenth-century Venice (in 1586 there were 1,694 Jews in a population of 149,000), the government still felt it was necessary to introduce measures to prevent the Catholic foundations of the republic from being undermined by the alien minority. In 1516 the Ghetto was introduced. Intended to minimize contacts with Christians, Jews were now crowded into a confined site without the right to own their dwellings. The regulations restricted freedom of movement to other parts of the city; between dusk and dawn the Ghetto gates were closed. Lay magistrates were appointed to supervise the Ghetto, observing Christians who entered it and spying on the activities of Jews who left it. They also enforced the medieval Church's rule for distinctive Jewish clothing: in Venice Jews were made easier to recognize by a circle of yellow cloth sewn to the outer garment, soon replaced by the more prominent yellow headgear. Sexual relations between Christians and Jews was regarded as a serious offence, and magistrates were empowered to prosecute in such cases, and also to punish blasphemy, a crime for which Jews were held to be prone. It is difficult to say how rigorously these strict measures were enforced. The officials were sometimes lax judging from the debate in the Venetian senate in March 1556 when there were complaints about Jews 'going where they please by night or day, staying in Christian houses'.

The Venetian Inquisition, a peculiar hybrid of lay and ecclesiastical officials, sometimes persecuted Jews, but its main concern was with baptized heretics. It was particularly alert to Christians fraternizing with the residents of the Ghetto. The Jews needed to employ gentile menial labour especially on the sabbath, to perform work on the day of rest. This the Venetian authorities allowed provided the workers left at night and took neither food nor drink from their Jewish employers. Research by Pullan (1971) on the Venetian Inquisition has revealed the flouting of these regulations in the 1580s in cases which show that for some Christians the Ghetto had a strong fascination. Valeria Brugnaleschi, a physician's widow, confessed to living in the Ghetto, enjoying Jewish food, and allegedly stated that their religion 'is better than ours'. When she subsequently brought a Jew to her home to perform 'magic rituals', she was punished with a public whipping and five years' banishment. Giorgio Moretto, a sailor, was one of several Christians who were drawn to the Jewish festivities which coincided with the period of Lent. While the Christians were tense, solemn and self-denying, the Jews were celebrating Purim, commemorating the life of Esther with jubilation in the synagogues, plays, feasts and weddings. Moretto participated in the merriment, breaking the Christian dietary laws by eating meat during **Lent**, and became infatuated with a Jewish girl. Arrested by the inquisition, he was warned to keep away from the Ghetto. Within two months he was back there again jokingly sporting a yellow Jewish hat. He was sentenced to three years on the galleys.

But for the bulk of Venice's Christians the Jews were viewed with contempt. They were charged with perverse obstinacy in refusing to embrace Christianity, blamed for the crucifixion of Jesus, and during the wars with the Ottoman Empire reviled as Turkish spies. In 1571 when Venetian Cyprus fell to the Turks, senators blamed Venice's Jewish inhabitants, accusing them of treachery, causing the grain shortage and the fire at the Arsenal and, by their money-lending, leading

youth into vice and reducing noble families to penury. One senator appealed for toleration because the Jews were useful to the economy, saved Christians from committing the sin of usury, and might one day convert. The senate voted to expel the Jews, but soon reversed that decision because of the potential loss of trade and income to the treasury from the special tax paid by Jews.

Yet for all these molestations and uncertainties, life for the Jews in Venice was far preferable to their recent experiences in other parts of Europe. For that reason David de' Pomi, a Jewish physician who sought refuge in Venice in the 1560s from the Papal States, wrote a treatise in praise of the Venetian constitution, ascribing a divine origin to it; so did the late sixteenth-century Venetian rabbi Leone de Modena.

The benefits included freedom of public worship; in 1528 the first of several Venetian synagogues with splendid interiors was built. And in 1570 Jewish attendance at Christian sermons aimed at conversion, compulsory in Rome, was officially rejected in Venice. Marranos, Jews of Portuguese origin who had been obliged in Antwerp to adopt a Christian façade, were permitted to revert to Judaism in Venice, though not until 1589 and after years of hounding by the inquisition.

Venetian Jews were encouraged to engage in lucrative international trade, especially with the Levant, but within the city they were prohibited from practising crafts and reduced to selling second-hand clothes and their main function, money-lending, particularly to the poor. Jewish doctors were in demand and enjoyed exceptional privileges. At Padua, on Venetian mainland territory, there was the only university in Europe open to Jews. This was the leading medical school in the West, attracting students from all over Europe. Its Jewish graduates who practised in Venice were exempted from wearing distinctive Jewish clothing and allowed free movement within the city. They attended nobles and prelates. Abraham de Balmes was physician to Domenico Grimani (1461–1523), son of a doge, and himself a cardinal and avid collector of antiquities and paintings. Grimani patronized Balmes's translations of medieval Arabic medical works from existing Hebrew versions into Latin. Jacob Mantino (d.1549), another Jewish graduate of Padua and of Spanish origin, attended Venetian nobles and later served as physician to the Venetian consul in Aleppo. He also translated numerous medical and philosophical works from Hebrew into

Latin, including Maimonides and Arabic authors like Averroës.

This was a traditional Jewish function of cultural mediation; it had been an important means of acquiring Greek and Arabic scientific wisdom in the medieval Latin West. Now it was continuing in Venice, though much of the knowledge disseminated was no longer new. Intermediaries between East and West also through trade, Jewish art dealers in Venice supplied antiquities from the Levant; in this way Cosimo de' Medici acquired in 1561 a magnificent collection of ancient coins.

Within Venice there were many signs of cultural exchange between Christian and Jew. Renaissance humanism touched Jewish scholars like Elijah Bahur (b.1469), a poet and grammarian of German origin whose epic poems in Yiddish were strongly influenced by Ariosto. Jewish humanists served as tutors to the wealthier Jewish families. And Jewish portrait painting, in the past often prohibited by rabbinical strictures against representational art, also found a clientele. Moses da Castellazzo (d.1525) was one such artist, but none of his works have survived.

Jewish performances during Purim of plays about Esther and Haman were presented to Venetian nobles in 1559, but on other occasions the authorities prohibited attendance by Christian audiences. Jewish musicians and dancers taught and entertained Venetians in spite of the republic's mid-fifteenth-century order to close such schools because of the increased opportunities for undesirable fraternization. By the 1590s a greater toleration prevailed, and Don Livio was authorized to take his company of Jewish dancers to perform in the houses of patricians.

But the strongest Christian interest in Jewish culture concerned Hebrew language and literature. Hebrew had always been important to Christian theologians because of the Jewish roots of Christianity. To this motive was now added the Renaissance passion for ancient languages and wisdom. Hebrew teachers were in demand. Government officials like Lorenzo Massa, secretary to the magistracy, was keen to learn Hebrew. Conte Guido Rangoni, condottiere (military contractor), took lessons from the Jewish physician Jacob Mantino. Such was the demand in Venice that Elijah Halfon, physician and rabbi, felt the need to write on the licitness of teaching Hebrew to gentiles, since the most revered Jewish texts like the Torah had traditionally been regarded as confined to Jews.

The great focus of interest was the doctrines of Cabbala ('tradition') contained in the *Sefer Ha-Zohar* ('Book of Splendour'), a thirteenth-century Castilian work purporting to contain the profoundest religious secrets transmitted orally from Moses. This was the mystical strand within Judaism, paralleling analogous Christian productions which may well have had the same Neoplatonic parentage. The *Zohar*'s depiction of God as incomprehensible and infinite, related to the created world like the centre point of a circle to the circumference, would have been familiar enough to Christian scholars. Similarly familiar would have been the *Zohar*'s central idea of emanations from the invisible deity expressed in such typical Neoplatonic terms as the transmission of light, the flow of water from a source, or the generation of a line from a mathematical point.

According to the *Zohar* there were ten emanations in the universe representing different aspects of God, and together they constituted a complex divine organism sometimes depicted as a branching tree or candelabra. This signified an active God within the created universe. Each emanation, or *Sefiroth* as they were called, was given a Hebrew name signifying God's 'love', 'power', 'compassion', 'majesty'. Through meditation on these names the devout was promised the discovery of hidden correspondences with biblical texts which opened the door to the perception of God's operations. Here use was made of ancient Jewish numerology, for Hebrew letters are also numbers. An idea of the technique can be grasped from an illustration of a fifteenth-century Florentine Hebrew manuscript in which the words of Psalm 67 are arranged in the form of a branching candelabra (Kedourie, 1979, p.198, fig. 18). Each of the words is translated into numbers and the sum added; the numerical answer was found to be equivalent to the letters of the name of God. Full of allegory and elaborate symbolism, the followers of Cabbala sought the characteristic goal of the mystic: ecstatic communion with God. For some there was the additional prize of magical control over nature, because the *Zohar* taught that the actions of the devout could restore harmony to the universe.

Venice was an important centre for cabbalistic studies, and there is ample evidence that Christian scholars there also took a serious interest. When the Venetian priest Joannes Pantheus published an alchemical work in Venice (1518), it included the Hebrew word for 'matter' and the arithmetical exercise of adding up the numerical values of the constituent letters. This illustrates the appeal of Cabbala for Renaissance practitioners of magic. There was also a religious reason for Christian Cabbalism. When the French scholar Guillaume Postel (1510–81) came into contact with the *Zohar* during his stay in Venice, he translated the work, convinced that the symbolic candelabra represented the light of Jesus Christ. And Faustino Tasso, a Venetian Franciscan, believed that the *Zohar* 'demonstrated the mystery of the Trinity as well as any Christian theologian'. It seemed that the conversion of the Jews might be achieved through their own books!

The new demand for Hebrew literature was reflected in the activity of Venice's Hebrew printing press, the most important in Europe. The production involved close collaboration of Christians and Jews. The principal promoter was Daniel Bomberg, a Christian from Antwerp who established a Hebrew press in Venice employing Jewish editors and proof-readers. Between 1516 and 1549 Bomberg's press issued 200 printings of fine books including the rabbinical Bible and the first complete edition of the Talmud. Hebrew type had first been used in Portugal. In Venice there is evidence that Christian type-cutters had to consult Jews on the correct forms of the letters; Master Leon, a Jewish second-hand clothes dealer, provided this service for Guillaume le Bé, a French type-cutter working in a Hebrew press set up near the Rialto in 1545 by Marcantonio Giustiniani, a Venetian noble. Bomberg's Hebrew type was later used in Antwerp by Plantin for his Hebrew Bible.

Bomberg's press was tolerated only by making payments to the government. When in 1525 his licence expired, his offer to the Venetian senate of 100 ducats was rejected with the criticism that his Jewish publications were undermining Catholicism. Raising his offer to 500 ducats caused the senate to withdraw its objections. But in 1553 Venice's Jewish presses (Bomberg's had by then closed) suffered severe financial losses as a result of government assaults. This was a consequence of Counter-Reform, Rome's harsher policy which included a call for the destruction of the Talmud, the post-biblical basis of Jewish law and tradition, supposedly blasphemous and preventing the Jews from accepting Christ. In Venice magistrates ordered raids on presses, the Ghetto and Christian houses in search of copies of the Talmud. In October the confiscated piles were burned in the Piazza San Marco. A further outbreak of intolerance with more burnings of various Jewish books

occurred in 1568; the reason is not clear but may have been due to official fear that the literature was politically subversive. Towards the end of the century Venice's Hebrew press had revived.

11 FRIAR FRANCESCO GIORGI: THE STRANGE SUCCESS OF A PHILOSOPHICAL HERETIC

STUART BROWN

Antwerp and Venice were, as you have seen, important centres for publishing books during our period. One way of comparing them, therefore, is to ask the following questions. First, how easy was it to have books published there? Second, what constraints were there on publishing new or unorthodox ideas in each case? Both places were centres which published books that came to be regarded as dangerous. But perhaps it is only in the case of Venice that this throws much light on the city itself. Antwerp, for example, published many books by one of the most radical philosophical figures of the sixteenth century, Heinrich Cornelius Agrippa, whom we shall be looking at in Block III, Section 13. Agrippa seems to have settled in Antwerp for a few years (*c*.1528–33), partly with the intention of making some money out of writing books. He met with some success in this regard, but one of his books included a very severe attack on the inquisition (see *Anthology* III.10). Agrippa's patron, the Holy Roman Emperor (Charles V), was turned against him and ordered him to be imprisoned. He was charged with heresy, and though he managed to escape from Antwerp, Agrippa seems thereafter to have been under frequent threat of arrest by the inquisition.

This story does not tell us much about the ethos of Antwerp as distinct from many other towns in the Holy Roman Empire. Venice, as a city-state, was in this respect more of a law to itself. It was, as we shall see, by no means a haven for those with unorthodox ideas. But it was possible for someone with unorthodox ideas to find a niche for himself in Venice. This section is a case study of a Franciscan friar who managed to do just that – Francesco Giorgi (1466–1540).

One respect in which Giorgi was unusual was in the interest he had in the Jewish Cabbala. As you will recall from Section 10, social and cultural contacts between the Jewish and Christian populations of Venice were strictly

Figure 25   Title page (with handwritten comments by the censor) of Francesco Giorgi, De harmonia mundi totius cantica tria…, *Venice, 1525. Reproduced by permission of the British Library Board.*

regulated. But, as we shall see in this section, Giorgi had a number of contacts among the rabbis and indeed was himself a Christian Cabbalist.

Cabbalism included in part a set of spiritual techniques for understanding and deriving other benefits from a study of the Bible. The Christian Cabbalists were not merely scholars but concerned about the revitalization of Christianity. They had, before Giorgi, included influential figures such as Cardinal Viterbo. The movement was later to fall under the suspicion of heresy and was largely (though never wholly) suppressed after the Reformations. But Giorgi had the good fortune to flourish during the period when the way of thinking of which it was a part was both acceptable and, up to a point, influential.

Those Christians who looked to the Cabbala for inspiration tended to approach it with a number of assumptions that were characteristic of Neoplatonism. They assumed that important spiritual truths, for instance, were known by the ancient sages of many different cultures, Greek, Egyptian and Babylonian as well as

Hebrew. One use of the Cabbala was to interpret Moses as having a similar philosophy to Plato, whom the Christian Cabbalists tended to think of as the Greek Moses. In the early pages of what is a classic of Neoplatonism, Giorgi insists that Plato is divinely inspired, indeed that he is nothing other than 'Moses speaking in the language of the Athenians'.

Giorgi's main book, entitled *De harmonia mundi* ('On the Harmony of the World'), was first published at Venice in 1525. (A French translation appeared in Paris in 1578.) A short chapter from this work is included in *Anthology* II.10. I suggest you read it now.

Figure 26   Diagram (man in a circle) from p.183 of Francesco Giorgi, L'Harmonie du monde, *1578. Reproduced by permission of the British Library Board.*

EXERCISE

1   What is Giorgi's main conclusion?

2   How does Giorgi argue for the truth of his main conclusion?

3   How does Giorgi argue for his interpretation of Moses?

DISCUSSION

1   Giorgi's main conclusion is that the whole universe is contained in Man. (More specifically, he argues that the universe is comprised of matter – 'dust' in the Book of Genesis – and spirit. God made Man out of the dust of the earth and breathed the spirit of life into Him.)

2   His argument is based on the authority of the ancient sages he cites. Since they agree that Man contains all things, Giorgi takes it to be so.

3   Giorgi concedes, in effect, that Moses does not say, in so many words, that Man contains all things. His meaning, on the contrary, is given 'secretly'. Giorgi fills out his interpretation of Moses partly by (what I hoped you might have guessed was) a cabbalistic argument based on the Hebrew letters of the word ADAM (which is the Hebrew for MAN). He also invites his reader at the outset to endorse his claim that Moses was 'an excellent philosopher', and in this way to secure a sympathetic reception for his suggestion that Moses' thought was in harmony with that of the other excellent philosophers he mentions.

I doubt if you were convinced by these arguments. Nowadays, I should add, such cabbalistic arguments are unlikely to impress biblical scholars. But what is of relevance from our point of view is not only the mode of argumentation but also the conclusion itself. For the thought that all things are contained in Man, that Man therefore is a microcosm of the whole universe, is one aspect of the overall harmony of the world that Giorgi's book was concerned to explain. Belief in universal harmony is one of the most characteristic thoughts of Neoplatonism and was taken by Giorgi and others to have many implications that we would find surprising. For instance Plato, in his *Timaeus*, had taught that God had created a perfect universe and, moreover, one that was perfectly orderly and harmonious. The Neoplatonists took Plato to be a follower of Pythagoras and supposed that the harmony of the world had a numerical basis. Certain proportions and certain numbers, it was believed, had a special religious significance and so played a key role in the theories of harmony that the Neoplatonists elaborated.

Such ideas were quite widely accepted, and the Neoplatonists not only supposed themselves to be, but were acknowledged as, authorities on all matters to do with harmony. This is part of the background to a remarkable episode in Giorgi's life (discussed in Radio 5, 'Giorgi') when he was used as just such an expert to advise on the building of a church in Venice and to help resolve a disagreement as to the proper proportions between the different parts of the building.

As well as being recognized as an authority on harmony, Giorgi was also well known as a Hebrew scholar and as someone in touch with leading Jewish authorities on the Old Testament. His expertise or his connections or both were regarded as sufficient to warrant a

secret envoy from the English king, Henry VIII, being dispatched to Venice to recruit his assistance.

Henry VIII had been married to Catherine of Aragon, his deceased brother's wife. A papal dispensation was required for this marriage. Marrying one's brother's widow was taken to be prohibited by the book of Leviticus 18:16, although it was actually required by the book of Deuteronomy 25:5–6 if the brother's widow had borne him no children. By 1529 Henry had decided he wanted a divorce and found himself needing to appeal to other authorities on the interpretation of Scripture than the pope. There were no Jews living openly in England at this time, and the suggestion of Thomas Cranmer that leading Jewish rabbis be consulted would have required sending abroad for their opinion. Richard Croke, who had been Henry's teacher of Greek, was sent to Venice to secure the assistance of Giorgi.

Giorgi was happy to co-operate and secured for Henry the advice he sought from the Jewish scholars with whom Giorgi was acquainted. According to Cecil Roth:

> This versatile scholar had little difficulty in finding Jewish scholars who were willing to support the English thesis, for there was an increasing tendency in Jewish life to evade the Deuteronomical prescription of a levirate marriage by the legal formality of the so-called *Halizah* ceremony (laid down as an alternative in Deuteronomy 25:7–10).
>
> (Roth, 1959, p.160)

Henry seems to have been grateful for the advice that Giorgi, as a result of his mission, was able to supply. He took the trouble to write in person to thank Giorgi for his assistance.

It may have struck you that it is really rather surprising that Giorgi, as a Franciscan friar, should have agreed to be involved in doing a favour for a remote monarch who was attempting to circumvent the pope's refusal to grant him a divorce. Giorgi was an active party in a project whose purpose was, in effect, subversive of papal authority. His motives are not known. Giorgi did, however, enjoy the confidence of the doge and was called upon to perform various services, including secret diplomatic missions, on behalf of the doge. It is possible that he was encouraged by the doge to do this favour for Henry VIII, and virtually certain that he would not have agreed to do it unless he believed the doge would approve. The story might then suggest that the doge and Venice were at least independent of – and perhaps not even well-disposed towards – the pope.

You may recall from Block I, Section 12 how the Florentine Neoplatonists like Ficino and Pico enjoyed the patronage and protection of their prince. Giorgi's position in Venice was perhaps rather similar. It was not that Venice was a particularly tolerant place. In 1516, nine years before Giorgi wrote *On the Harmony of the World*, there had been the furore over Pomponazzi's *On the Immortality of the Soul*. Pomponazzi was a teacher at Padua within the territory of Venice. It was the Venetian clergy who persuaded the doge to order his book to be burned and to initiate proceedings for heresy against Pomponazzi. On this occasion it was the pope who took what we would call the 'liberal' view not only by insisting that the proceedings be dropped, but also by encouraging Pomponazzi and his opponents to continue their debate through further publications.

If Venice was not a particularly tolerant place, Giorgi was not merely tolerated but flourished. But Christian Cabbalists like him were increasingly liable to be harassed and persecuted during waves of anti-semitism (see Block III, Section 13).

The late Dame Frances Yates (*Supplememtary Texts* 4) suggested that the history of Giorgi's changing reputation reflected the changing times. She drew attention to the disapproval by a later censor of Giorgi's *De harmonia mundi*: 'This work is full of the arguments of Platonists and Cabalists (*sic*) … It is therefore to be read with caution.'

Part of what was objectionable about these arguments is evident in the passage from Giorgi's book in the *Anthology* II.10. Giorgi there argues for his conclusions by saying, in effect, that they are matters on which the wise men of the past (Moses, Plato, Hermes Trismegistus and so on) all agree. Yet underlying this argument is the assumption that truth is by no means a monopoly but something that, on the contrary, we might expect to find shared amongst the wise in many different cultures. Moreover, Giorgi assumed this was so in religious matters. Such an attitude might naturally be accompanied by a relatively tolerant view of other cultures, and even the acknowledgement that different religions have access to some part at least of the truth. By the end of the sixteenth century such attitudes are hard to find. Whereas Giorgi might defer to the religious authority of rabbis

and pagan philosophers, the rivalries and schisms within Christendom made those who were party to them more inclined to claim a monopoly for what they claimed as the authoritative source of religious truth. It became unthinkable that a good Catholic should be involved in a scheme to trump papal authority by appealing to the judgement of Jewish religious teachers. But it seems to have been entirely thinkable for a Venetian in 1529. The pious Francesco Giorgi, in his special historical situation, was not only involved in such a scheme but, for all we know to the contrary, had a completely clear conscience about it.

12 CONCLUSION

LUCILLE KEKEWICH

You should now have a good idea of the physical environment of Venice and Antwerp. In the public places of both cities the Christian, propertied men pursued their business, intellectual stimulation and pleasure. Others were less privileged: women were expected to confine their activities to their homes and to low-profile piety in church; the poor were excluded from public life except as recipients of charity or harsh justice; Jews enjoyed a precarious toleration.

The themes of the course are traced through the differences between the cities. The papacy still enjoyed considerable temporal power in Italy which created conflict with Venice. On doctrinal issues, however, there was little sign of unorthodoxy, a contributory factor to Venetian political stability. In Antwerp, on the other hand, religious ferment was closely associated with political instability. This was a popular manifestation of religious fervour rather than an attempt to secularize society. Members of guilds and confraternities engaged in religious processions and patronage of works of art in the early part of the century with an enthusiasm only equal to that with which they demolished statues of the Virgin and altarpieces after the impact of the Protestant Reformation.

Antwerp had a long tradition of flouting lawful political authority. The troubles it encountered in the second part of the century arose not only from religious strife. Until the reign of Philip II it had always been ruled by north European princes; many spent part of their time in the Low Countries and had some understanding of the needs of the people. The influx of Spanish officials who drained away

Antwerp's wealth in taxation and attempted to enforce the Catholic Reformation drove its inhabitants into rebellion.

Traditional Catholic intellectual authority, as Block I has shown, had already been called in question by Renaissance scholarship. Pensionary Pauwels, who preferred Lorenzo Valla and Roman history to the commentaries of the Church Fathers, is instructive. Yet Bessarion's collection showed that it was possible to embrace the new learning without heresy. More dangerous was the fascination that the Jewish Cabbala writings held for Christian scholars. In the early part of the century, before the Catholic Reformation organized its sanctions, Francesco Giorgi got away with expressing opinions similar to those which later caused Giordano Bruno to be burnt at the stake.

A case study of two great cities might be expected to address the issues of regionalism, which is another course theme. Venice and Antwerp both expressed enormous civic pride and affirmed a cultural identity in their proclamations, processions, religious festivals and patronage of art; yet both were very cosmopolitan in comparison to most parts of western Europe. Both cities give a good insight into the widening perspectives of Europeans in the sixteenth century. Both were favourably situated to take advantage of the enormous expansion of overseas exploration and trade, Venice the more so. Antwerp, damaged by decades of political turmoil and boxed up in the Scheldt, had to watch great Atlantic powers such as England and Spain divide the spoils.

We suggest that you now turn to TBC 2A and the accompanying notes in the *Cassette Handbook*.

BIBLIOGRAPHY

Burke, P. (1974) *Venice and Amsterdam*, Temple Smith.

Geanokoplos, D.J. (1963) *Greek Scholars in Venice*, Cambridge, Mass.

Kedourie E. (ed.) (1979) *The Jewish World*, Thames and Hudson.

Krahn, C. (1936) *Menno Simons, 1496–1561*, Karlsruhe.

Lane, F.C. (1973) *Venice: A Maritime Republic*, Baltimore.

Pullan, B. (1971) *Rich and Poor in Renaissance Venice*, Basil Blackwell.

Ramsay, G.D. (1975) *The City of London*, Manchester.

Rapp, R.T. (1976) *Industry and Economic Decline in Seventeenth-Century Venice*, Cambridge, Mass. and London.

Roth, C. (1959) *The Jews in the Renaissance*, Harper Torchbooks.

Vast, H. (1878) *Le Cardinal Bessarion, 1403–72*, Paris.

Voet, L. (1973) *Antwerp: The Golden Age*, Antwerp.